IMAGES
of America

CHRYSLER HERITAGE

A PHOTOGRAPHIC HISTORY

Son of a Kansas railroad locomotive engineer, Walter P. Chrysler (1875–1940) was a self-made multi-millionaire captain of industry when this 1925 photo was taken in the study of his Long Island, New York, home. Chrysler quit high school to become an apprentice locomotive mechanic and—for the first 15 years of his career—moved around from one prairie or mountain state railroad roundhouse to another, sharpening his skills at solving mechanical problems and managing work crews. His big break came in 1909 when he moved from railroad maintenance in Iowa to locomotive manufacturing in Pittsburgh. From his successes there, Chrysler was mentored by a Boston investment banker into Buick Motor Company, which he quickly rose to head as a General Motors vice president. He retired a wealthy man at the age of 45. Soon his banker friends summoned him to save the Willys-Overland and Maxwell-Chalmers automobile companies. He converted Maxwell to Chrysler Corporation with a new car featuring advanced engineering. Walter P. Chrysler saw his namesake company rise to number two in the industry before retiring from active management in 1935. (C)

IMAGES
of America

CHRYSLER HERITAGE
A PHOTOGRAPHIC HISTORY

Michael W.R. Davis

ARCADIA
PUBLISHING

Published by Arcadia Publishing
Charleston, South Carolina

Printed in the United States of America

Library of Congress Catalog Card Number: 00107787

For all general information contact Arcadia Publishing at:
Telephone 843-853-2070
Fax 843-853-0044
E-mail sales@arcadiapublishing.com
For customer service and orders:
Toll-Free 1-888-313-2665

Visit us on the Internet at www.arcadiapublishing.com

Lee (for Lido) A. Iacocca (1924–), son of Italian immigrants in a Pennsylvania steel town, graduated from Lehigh and Princeton. He joined Ford Motor Company in 1946 as a steel-mill-engineering trainee, but soon switched to sales. After 12 years working with dealers, he moved to the company's headquarters, where he quickly rose to head Ford Division—and fathered the Mustang. Iacocca rode such triumphs to the company's presidency, but after more than 20 years of meteoric performance, was dismissed by Chairman Henry Ford II in 1978. Chrysler Corporation, then in financial shambles, was quick to hire him. He became Chrysler's savior, negotiating a Federal Government loan guarantee. With the help of trusted aides brought from Ford, Iacocca revamped Chrysler's products, starting with the 1981 K-car, which spawned a variety of new models including the Minivan. Like Walter P. Chrysler, he participated in advertisements, best known for his challenge: "If you can find a better car, buy it." In this scene, he dramatically unveiled the K-car long before its availability for purchase, building public confidence in the company and desire for the product. (C)

CONTENTS

In the latter part of the 19th century steam engines and electricity were the technological marvels of the age. Steam locomotives, steamboats, and electric streetcars were supplanting ages-old foot and animal power. Walter P. Chrysler (center) posed here with fellow mechanics in front of a locomotive at a Kansas roundhouse sometime in the 1890s. His conversion subsequently from maintaining and fixing mechanical devices to large-scale manufacturing, from railroad technology to automotive technology, came naturally. (H)

INTRODUCTION

"Success has many fathers, failure is an orphan," goes the old saying, and it aptly applies to the Chrysler Heritage. This volume relates some of the stories of those automotive successes, fathers, failures, and orphans.

Note that I write "heritage" and not "history." Chrysler "history" would encompass only that of Walter P. Chrysler and the Chrysler Corporation. However, more than any other automobile company surviving—almost—to the end of the motorcar's first century, Chrysler epitomizes both the cyclical boom-and-bust economic character of the automotive industry and its core in the Motor City, Detroit.

Chrysler's heritage was to rise in the mid-20s from the ashes of failed and abandoned auto companies in the early years of the industry and then experience a seemingly unending cycle of wealth and poverty for the next 75 years. Unlike General Motors with its Flint heritage and Ford with its longtime home in Dearborn, Chrysler has always been more a Detroit-centered company, even though its headquarters was in Highland Park, an industrial suburb completely surrounded by Detroit. Chrysler's key assembly plants—Plymouth, Dodge, DeSoto, and Chrysler—were encircled by Detroit's city limits for several decades.

Today, in 2001, Chrysler's future is clouded by its 1998 merger with Daimler-Benz of Germany—now looked upon by many as more of a takeover. For those of us with long memories, there is a supreme irony in this because of Chrysler's leading role in World War II's winning Arsenal of Democracy.

My family contributed its part to Chrysler's prosperity over many years. In World War I, my father—a sergeant-first-class in the American Expeditionary Force in France—commanded a crew of Dodge ambulances (p. 25). As a consequence, after he learned to drive at the age of 35 (!) in 1922, Dad's first new car was a 1924 Dodge. During the 1930s, my great-uncle Damon, more like a grandfather to me, bought a new Plymouth sedan every couple of years, and another uncle, who owned a greenhouse, always came down from the country in his Plymouth pickup truck.

In 1945, Uncle Damon died, leaving his black 1941 Plymouth Special Deluxe four-door sedan to my mother—and I taught myself to drive in that car at the age of 14. After new cars became available in the post-war years, my father owned a succession of Chrysler products—'48 DeSoto, '50 Chrysler, '52 Dodge, '53 Dodge, '55 Dodge. My sister and her husband had a '47 Plymouth followed by a '52 DeSoto. I drove a '49 Plymouth during my college years, and my first new car was a '55 Plymouth coupe with the new V-8 engine. I put more than 100,000 miles on it and kept it as a second car for some time after I went to work for Ford Motor Company in 1960.

My connection with Chrysler products doesn't end there, though. In 1972, on a used-car lot, I saw a 1941 Plymouth nearly identical to the one in which I had learned to drive. So I bought it with some of my Ford earnings, had it overhauled and then taught my three children how to drive in it. We lovingly called it "Uncle D," after my great-uncle, and I kept it for 15 years.

As I pointed out in the introduction to *General Motors: A Photographic History* (the first in this series), Detroit is a small town in many ways, where we who have worked in the auto industry tend to know many of our competitors personally. The auto industry is supremely competitive, much driven by the pride that comes from outmatching those industry rivals we know so well. Nevertheless, there is an overriding solidarity and pride in industry accomplishments, and I am glad to be a herald of Chrysler's.

–Michael W.R. Davis
Royal Oak, Michigan
January 2001

EDITORIAL POSTSCRIPT:

When providing sales comparison information, I have normally used new car registrations, because they are more available, more consistent and more reliable than either production numbers, factory sales or reported retail sales. For product identification and comparisons, I have used wheelbase.

Following is the key to photo credits and sources in parentheses at the end of each caption:

A	Chrysler Corporation Annual Reports
B	Larry Gustin, Buick Public Relations
C	DaimlerChrysler Corporate Historical Collection
D	Michael W. R. Davis, personal collection
E	ESD/Engineering Society of Detroit
F	Chrysler Corporation/DaimlerChrysler Product Communications
G	Gulfstream Aerospace, General Dynamics Corporation
H	Walter P. Chrysler Boyhood Home & Museum
K	Jack Kausch Photography
M	Detroit Historical Museum, City of Detroit
N	National Automotive History Collection, Detroit Public Library
P	Petersen Publishing Company
R	Walter P. Reuther Library, Wayne State University
S	National Atomic Museum, Kirtland Air Force Base
U	U.S. Merchant Marine Academy

One

WHY DETROIT?

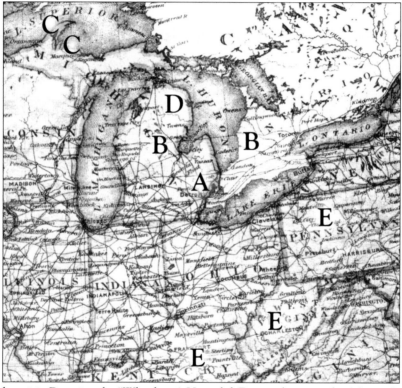

People who visit Detroit ask, "Why here? How did Detroit become the Motor City?" One answer, geography, is illustrated by this late 19th-century map which shows Detroit (A) in the midst of the Great Lakes system then dominating transportation. Detroit was also served by multiple rail lines heading east, west, and south. Moreover, the needed natural resources were accessible—hardwood forests in northern Michigan and Ontario (B), iron and copper in Michigan's Upper Peninsula (C), limestone in Michigan's Northeast (D), and coal not too far away by rail and water in Pennsylvania, West Virginia, and Kentucky (E). Other factors are considered in the pages following: relevant manufacturing and men willing to take personal or financial risks. Timing, interest and luck also played roles in why neither Chicago, Milwaukee, Toledo, Cleveland, nor Buffalo—all on the Great Lakes, too—put it all together to challenge Detroit successfully for the Motor City title. (D)

For several decades prior to the beginnings of the automobile industry, Detroit was home to large railroad equipment enterprises where workers and management alike developed skills in heavy-wheeled vehicle manufacture. This 1889 view of the Michigan Car Company Shops in Detroit even shows moving assembly lines. (M)

Railroad cars manufactured in Detroit required factories that could produce heavy castings for railroad wheels and axles, as shown in this 1889 view at the Detroit Car Wheel Foundry. The know-how honed to build and operate such plants could be applied later to castings for automobiles and trucks. (M)

"The Home of Jewel Stoves, Ranges and Furnaces—the Largest Stove Plant in the World"
"More than 4,000,000 Stoves have been made in these Great Foundries"

DETROIT STOVE WORKS

As this turn-of-the-century advertising stated, the Detroit Stove Works on East Jefferson Avenue was "The home of Jewel Stoves, Ranges and Furnaces—the Largest Stove Plant in the World." The ad also bragged, "More than 4,000,000 Stoves have been made in these Great Foundries." (E)

In the 1890s, bicycling with the newly invented "safety bicycle" of even-sized wheels swept America. Detroit had several bicycle makers whose work with steel tubing, wire-spoke wheels, rubber tires, and chain drives would become applicable to automobiles. This Evans and Dodge bicycle was built by the Dodge brothers and a partner in a shop in Windsor, Ontario, across the river from Detroit. The brothers' next venture was a machine shop. (D)

Detroit's stoves such as this Jewel model produced by the factory shown on the opposite page required complicated iron castings. Design and mass-production expertise with these parts would prove useful as the infant auto industry grew. Engine blocks, axle casings, and transmission cases all were made of cast iron, requiring skilled metalworking craftsmanship. (E)

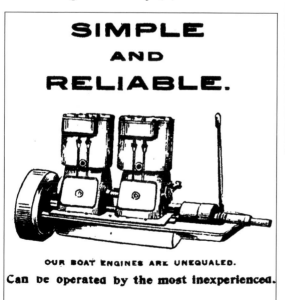

SIMPLE AND RELIABLE.

OUR BOAT ENGINES ARE UNEQUALED.

Can be operated by the most inexperienced.

Detroit (and other Great Lakes ports) had many boat works, large and small. The marine industry quickly saw the advantages—for small boats—of gasoline engines, like this Olds model, over steam engines. Liquid fuel was more convenient to store and use than coal or wood, and the compact gasoline engine mounted more easily in motor launches. (M)

The last decade of the 19th century witnessed a new phenomenon: development of internal-combustion gasoline-powered engines in place of bulky steam engines, at first designed for stationary applications like pumps. This 1900 advertisement for Olds Motor Works appeared before production of the Olds car actually began. The investors who provided capital for Ransom E. Olds' enterprise were heirs to a copper-mining fortune from Michigan's Upper Peninsula. Olds had first built a steam-powered car in his father's Lansing machine shop in 1892, later switching to gasoline engines. He incorporated the Motor Works in 1897, but did not start producing automobiles—the famous "curved dash" models—until 1901. A number of curious and energetic young men who went to work for Olds contributed to the Chrysler Heritage. (M)

Two

CHRYSLER PREDECESSORS

The first of the Motor City's automotive pioneers, Charles B. King (1868–1957) built and drove the first gasoline-powered motor car on the streets of Detroit on March 6, 1896, three months before Henry Ford's Quadricycle appeared. Here King is shown during the American automobile industry's Golden Anniversary in 1946, examining an exhibition photograph of himself and mechanic Oliver Barthel making that pioneering drive in Detroit—a familiar image in automotive histories. King dropped out of engineering studies at Cornell to work for the railcar shops of Michigan Car Company (p. 10). Exhibits at the Chicago World's Fair in 1893 got him interested in gasoline-powered motor cars. After 1896, King became involved in design and development of several cars—notably the Northern, Maxwell, and Thomas-Detroit, which became part of the Chrysler Heritage. (N)

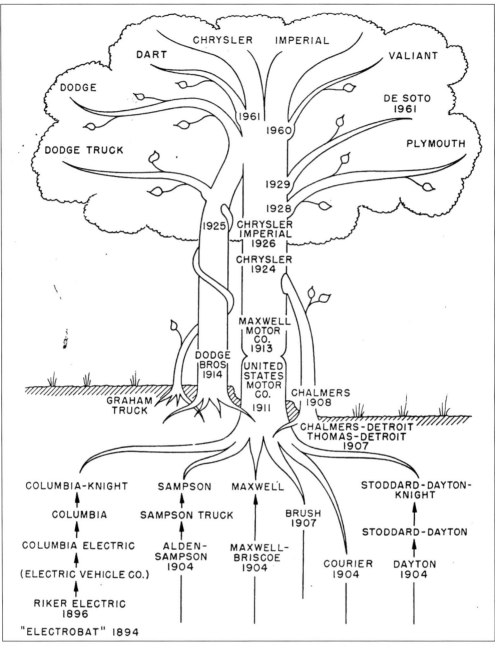

CHRYSLER   IMPERIAL

DART   VALIANT

DODGE

DE SOTO
1961

1961

1960

DODGE TRUCK   PLYMOUTH

1929

1928

1925 CHRYSLER
IMPERIAL
1926

CHRYSLER
1924

MAXWELL
MOTOR
CO.
1913

DODGE
BROS
1914   UNITED
STATES
MOTOR
CO.
1911   CHALMERS
1908

GRAHAM
TRUCK   CHALMERS-DETROIT
THOMAS-DETROIT
1907

COLUMBIA-KNIGHT   SAMPSON   MAXWELL   STODDARD-DAYTON-
KNIGHT

COLUMBIA   SAMPSON TRUCK   BRUSH
1907   STODDARD-DAYTON

COLUMBIA ELECTRIC   ALDEN-
SAMPSON
1904   MAXWELL-
BRISCOE
1904

(ELECTRIC VEHICLE CO.)   COURIER
1904   DAYTON
1904

RIKER ELECTRIC
1896

"ELECTROBAT" 1894

This early 1960s drawing of "Chrysler's Family Tree" is not entirely complete since it does not show the Northern, introduced in 1902 and designed by Jonathan D. Maxwell, who left for Maxwell-Briscoe two years later. The illustration also neglects the Dodge Brothers' key role in building engines, transmissions, and axles for Ford Motor Company prior to 1914. And at the time the "tree" was drawn, Jeep—today a strong plank in the DaimlerChrysler product line—was still two companies removed from the Chrysler Corporation. Nevertheless, the drawing provides a good map for the complicated automotive history of the Chrysler Heritage. It also identifies, unfortunately, a couple of '60s car lines and several long-standing Chrysler brands—Plymouth, DeSoto, Imperial—which became consigned to "history" themselves. (C)

14

In 1902, King and Maxwell, who worked together at Olds, started Northern Manufacturing Co., financed by William Barbour, president of Detroit Stove Works. By the time of this 1906 ad, three models were offered, at 7 hp, 20 hp, and 30 hp, all of opposed-cylinder engine designs like those of the VW Beetle and Subaru. Relatively quiet operation earned them the name "Silent Northern." (N)

The Thomas-Detroit car was the brainchild of two other graduates of Olds Motor Works: Roy Chapin and Howard Coffin. Founded in 1906 with an order from established Buffalo auto manufacturer E.R. Thomas for 500 cars, it became a predecessor of Chalmers. Chrysler's East Jefferson Plant had its beginning with Thomas-Detroit manufacture. Shown here are two 1907 models at a performance event in Savannah, Georgia. (N)

Roy D. Chapin (1880–1936), left, partnered with Howard E. Coffin (1873–1937) from the University of Michigan through Olds Motor Works, Thomas-Detroit, Chalmers-Detroit and, in 1909, the founding of Hudson Motor Car Company. Chapin began as an Olds photographer and test driver who found his real talent in sales and what today is called networking. Coffin was the engineer and inside man. (N)

Edwin R. Thomas (1850–1936), left, was heir to coal mining, steamboat, and railroad interests, but became interested in manufacturing bicycles in Toronto, then automobiles in Buffalo. Hugh Chalmers (1873–1932) became wealthy as general manager of National Cash Register Co. of Dayton. Chapin persuaded him to invest in Thomas-Detroit, which was renamed Chalmers-Detroit in 1908. (N)

16

This Chalmers-Detroit ran off a primitive road in Mexico during a Denver-to-Mexico City promotional tour in 1909. From the earliest days of motor cars to the present, auto manufacturers have favored attention-getting performance events to demonstrate their speed, economy, reliability, or durability. After such events, cars marked with their records would be circulated through dealer showrooms to attract customers. (N)

This 1910 photograph of a Chalmers touring car shows how—before closed cars became common and heaters were invented—motorists had to cope with winter weather by bundling up. Notice how little in appearance the Chalmers has changed from the Thomas-Detroit of 1906–1907 (p. 15). (N)

This view of the 6-cylinder Chalmers engine introduced in 1912—particularly when compared with engines of the '20s, '30s, '60s, and '80s pictured later in this volume—demonstrates what huge changes have taken place as automotive technology has developed. Note that each cylinder stands alone rather than being enclosed in a water-jacket block. (N)

In contrast, this photo of the body drop at the Chalmers assembly plant around 1914 seems to show, compared to a Dodge plant 50 years later (p. 88), that not much has changed. But there are two big differences: the moving assembly line and substitution of equipment for manual labor. Although Ford was perfecting moving assembly when this photo was taken, the technology had not yet been adopted elsewhere. (N)

A common belief is that women workers were not employed in auto company plants until World War II, when they were needed for war production to replace men called off to the armed services (p. 56). This *c.* 1914 photo of women employees in the Chalmers trim department demonstrates otherwise. However, men performed the dirtier, heavier duty work in foundries, machine shops, and assembly. (N)

During a 1915 Detroit streetcar strike, Chalmers Motor Company used its own fleet of Chalmers trucks to transport workers to and from rallying points near their homes. The multi-storied factory buildings in the background were typical of the time, and later served Chrysler into the 1990s as its East Jefferson Assembly Plant. For many years, the site was headquarters for the Chrysler-Plymouth Division. (N)

Jonathan D. Maxwell (1864–1928), left, was a machinist and designer who moved to Olds after working for Haynes, an automotive pioneer in Indiana. After helping found Northern (p. 15), in 1904 Maxwell introduced a car of his own design and name with support of the Briscoe brothers. Walter Flanders (1871–1923) was relatively late on the Detroit scene as a 1907 crankshaft supplier to Ford. Flanders later headed Maxwell and Chalmers. (N)

When introduced in 1904, the Maxwell car featured many advanced features, including front engine and honeycomb radiator. Twenty years later, a reworked Maxwell became the first Chrysler. Although designed in Detroit by J.D. Maxwell, the Maxwell car was built for about ten years at various other locations in the East and Midwest mostly under the umbrella of U.S. Motor Co., an unsuccessful General Motors copycat. (C)

Benjamin Briscoe (1869–1945), left, a successful supplier of sheet metal products to the stove industry and to infant car manufacturers, was an original investor in the Maxwell-Briscoe Co. Driving the '10 Brush Runabout here was his brother Frank (1875–1954), head of the Brush car company. Alanson Brush (1878–1952), right, was an inventor who worked for the Leland and Faulconer machine shop and Cadillac before joining with Frank Briscoe to produce the Brush Runabout in 1907. (N)

The one-story (unusual for the time) Brush Runabout factory shown here was erected in Highland Park, a suburb of Detroit completely enclosed by the big city. After the failure of U.S. Motors, in 1913 the plant became part of Maxwell and, eventually, Chrysler Corp. Both the first Detroit-made Maxwell and the first DeSoto were built here. (N)

The most remarkable thing about this 1916 Maxwell was not its unusual "baby buggy" canopy-type top, but rather its newly redesigned 4-cylinder engine. The Maxwell Four continued in service into the 1920s and—further refined by the new Chrysler Corporation's genius engineers—became the powerplant of the Chrysler Model 50 in 1926 (really a re-badged Maxwell) and the new Plymouth in 1928. (C)

By 1916, Maxwell was producing close to 50,000 cars a year and needed more facilities. Chalmers was producing half as many but had taken over and expanded the former Brush facility in Highland Park. Maxwell and Chalmers worked out an arrangement whereby Maxwell would manage Highland Park production and both makes also would be assembled at Chalmers' East Jefferson Plant. In this 1920 "birds-eye" illustration, the plant is labeled Maxwell. (N)

Before Walter P. Chrysler's arrival on the scene, the most important contributors to the Chrysler Heritage were the Dodge brothers, John (1864–1920), left, and Horace (1868–1920). They were so close that in life and death they were treated more as one person than two. Trained machinists, they first manufactured bicycles (p.11) and then turned to automotive parts—for Olds in 1901 and Ford in '03. (N)

The infant Ford Motor Company was short on cash and credit, so it paid the Dodges 50 shares of stock (10 percent of the capitalization) for producing engines. The Dodges rode Ford growth into the millions and built a huge plant in Hamtramck, like Highland Park, a city surrounded by Detroit. This view of the Dodge office building was taken *c.* 1915. (C)

By 1914, the Dodges already were millionaires from a combination of Ford stock dividends and building major components for Ford cars. They decided they could build a better car than the Model T, and here are shown riding in the first Dodge. In the background is John Dodge's home on Boston Boulevard near Woodward Avenue in Detroit. (C)

From the beginning the Dodges instituted a major innovation in motor-car development—a fairly elaborate test track behind the Hamtramck factory. New Dodges, most still lacking headlights, were driven up and down the artificial hill in the background to test performance and braking before being shipped to dealers. It paid off for Dodge with a reputation for durability at a time when purchasing most makes proved the maxim: "Buyer Beware." (C)

24

The Dodge reputation also got a huge boost when General John "Black Jack" Pershing ordered 150 cars for his cross-country U.S. Army expeditions against Mexican bandits along Southwestern borders in 1916. Here a "Pershing Dodge" is shown alongside an artillery piece. Pershing later became commander of U.S. forces in France during World War I, where his staff car was a Cadillac. (C)

As part of its contribution to the American crusade to "Save the World for Democracy," Dodge built ambulances like this, based on Dodge trucks which in turn were modified from cars. Dodge also contributed to the war effort by devising and producing recoil mechanisms for French heavy artillery pieces. The distinctive Dodge appearance, with headlamps level with the hood top, made a lasting "brand" impression on the public. (C)

Eight Billion Bottles

AMERICA'S enthusiasm for wholesome beverages has elevated the Bottler to a position of high rank among the country's leading industries. Last year 12,000 Bottlers put up approximately 8,000,000,000 bottles of soft drinks and mineral waters, which the public bought in 150,000 stores at a cost of $400,000,000. Bottlers employ 120,000 persons, pay $125,000,000 a year in wages and operate 60,000 trucks. The proportion of Graham Brothers Trucks among this fleet of 60,000 is increasing enormously every year—because Bottlers, particularly, require good trucks. And because, in this business, as in the 363 others in which Graham Brothers Truck is serving, owners are always impressed by its exceptional ability to give long service at low cost.

GRAHAM BROTHERS
Detroit - Evansville - Stockton - Toronto
A Division of Dodge Brothers, Inc.

The Graham brothers, from left, Robert (1885–1967), Joseph (1882–1970), and Ray (1887–1932), were sons of a prosperous Southern Indiana farmer who discovered gas on his property and used it to establish a glass bottle factory. After this business merged with Owens of Toledo in 1916, the sons developed a medium-duty truck using automotive components. In 1922, Dodge, having only a light truck line, arranged to sell Dodge-powered Graham trucks through its dealers. (C)

This 1925 advertisement for Graham Brothers' trucks indicates that the firm is a "Division of Dodge Brothers, Inc." The Dodge brothers had died separately in 1920, and hired managers were running their company. By the end of the decade, the Graham truck had become the Dodge truck, the Grahams having sold out their interests in 1927. (C)

Three

WALTER P. CHRYSLER TO THE RESCUE

Walter P. Chrysler stands proudly beside the first car bearing his name—the 1924 Chrysler introduced publicly in January at the New York Auto Show. WPC's first manufacturing job was as superintendent of the Pittsburgh American Locomotive (ALCO) plant in 1909, where he re-arranged the layout to provide for "progressive" manufacturing. Boston banker James Storrow, a director of both ALCO and General Motors, recommended Chrysler to Buick Motors in 1911. He became works manager there at $6,000 a year; a pay cut from ALCO. Over the next four years, he introduced numerous improvements to Buick production. WPC's reward from GM President William C. Durant was presidency of Buick in 1916 at a salary of $500,000 plus stock. He also was elected a GM vice president and director. (C)

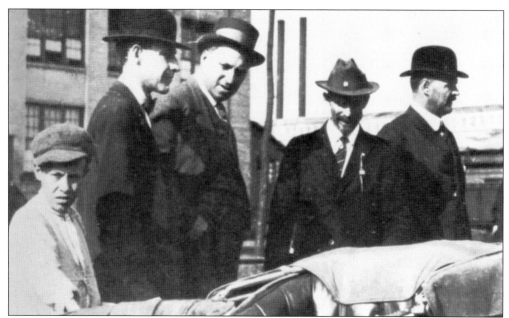

This may be the only known candid photo of Chrysler (center) at Buick. At the Flint Buick plant, WPC found skilled woodworkers (for the wooden bodies) but backwardness in metalworking. Under his direct management, Buick annual production rose from 13,389 to 128,632. In addition to solving production problems, he also brought costs under control. When WPC resigned from GM at the end of 1919, he was recruited by investment bankers to save Willys-Overland and then Maxwell. (B)

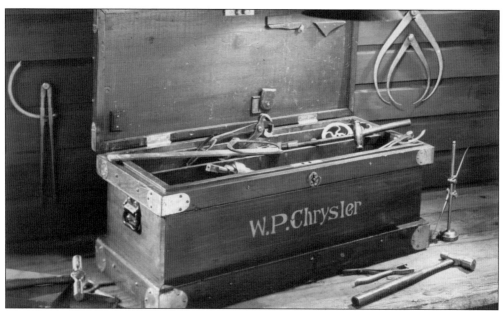

Chrysler never forgot his workingman origins and was proud of his skills as a mechanic, machinist, and fixer of mechanical things gone wrong. He dragged this toolbox—filled with hand-made tools from apprentice days—from roundhouses to locomotive works to auto plants. Today you can see it at the Chrysler Museum in Auburn Hills, Michigan. (C)

John North Willys (1873–1933) started as a bicycle salesman in Elmira, New York, before 1900 and became an Overland dealer in 1906. In a series of subsequent transactions, he gained control of the Overland Company, re-named it Willys-Overland, and expanded by buying other Ohio auto manufacturers. By 1915 Willys was second to Ford in sales. (C)

In 1920, when this smart Willys-Knight touring car was built, Willys-Overland was in trouble from overextended bank loans and weak sales in a post-war recession. Chrysler was brought in for $1 million a year salary to fix Willys, which he accomplished in a matter of months, proving he was a master of management as well as machinery. Then, in 1921, the bankers asked WPC to salvage Maxwell-Chalmers as well. (C)

The most important result of WPC's assignment to save Willys was his becoming acquainted with a trio of brilliant engineers under contract to Willys to develop a new 6-cylinder engine. Here they are pictured, from left to right, in 1928 with WPC and the Chrysler car powered by their engine: Chrysler, Carl Breer, Fred Zeder, and Owen Skelton. First year production for the new Chrysler car was 32,000. (C)

The new Zeder-Skelton-Breer Chrysler Six design, shown here, essentially stayed in production with only modest changes from 1923 to 1961. The high-compression 201-cid engine featured full-pressure lubrication and seven crankshaft bearings, producing 68 hp at 3,600 rpm. Significantly, it performed well and was steadfastly reliable. Chrysler Corporation was built upon this engine design and other engineering advances like hydraulic brakes. (C)

Before introducing the Chrysler Six in place of Chalmers, WPC managed to solve Maxwell's mechanical problems (mainly bad axles) and aggressively advertised the car as the "Good Maxwell," as in this advertisement. In short order, Chrysler Corporation replaced Maxwell Motor Corporation (which earlier had replaced Maxwell-Chalmers as the corporate entity) and the Maxwell car became the 4-cylinder Chrysler 50 series. (C)

This emblem, embossed onto the bright-metal radiator shell of the Chrysler car, became the symbol of the new Chrysler Corporation, incorporated on June 6, 1925. In the 1990s, the company revived the badge in modified design once again to label Chrysler cars. (D)

25 Miles *to the* Gallon

Startling good news to tens of thousands—the first announcements of the new good Maxwell's amazing results. Never since the Chrysler took the country by storm has the automobile industry known such whole-hearted response—such a dramatic and decisive triumph.

Not content with designing into this car power and pick-up equaled only in the higher priced fields, Chrysler engineering genius and fine manufacturing facilities enable the new good Maxwell owner to enjoy these performance advantages with unparalleled economy.

In almost sensationally low cost of operation and maintenance —as in speed and acceleration—this great car has written a wholly new page in motor car achievement, and in the accomplishment of the great organization which builds the Maxwell.

Balloon tires, natural wood wheels, stop-light, transmission lock, Duco finish standard on all Maxwell models. Shrouded visor integral with roof, heater, standard on all closed models.

Touring Car, $895; Club Coupe, $995; Club Sedan, $1045; Standard Four-Door Sedan, $1095; Special Four-Door Sedan, $1245. All prices f. o. b. Detroit, Tax extra.

There are Maxwell dealers and superior Maxwell service everywhere. All dealers are in position to extend the convenience of time-payments. Ask about Maxwell's attractive plan.

58 Miles *per* Hour

5 *to* 25 Miles *in* 8 Seconds

MAXWELL

The New Good
MAXWELL

Blessed by a booming economy with growing industry sales, WPC expanded his product offerings to match GM's "stair-step" marketing concept. At the entry level came the new Plymouth, a reworked Chrysler 50 powered by the old Maxwell Four. This shows the first Plymouth produced, at the old Maxwell plant in Highland Park on June 14, 1928. (C)

Almost concurrently with Plymouth, on August 4, 1928, Chrysler introduced the medium-priced DeSoto, which set a first-year medium-price sales record of 81,065 which stood for many years. Shown here is an $845 roadster. DeSoto was powered by a 175-cid Six, smaller and less robust than the Chrysler. (C)

At the same time he was developing the Plymouth and DeSoto, WPC was negotiating with bankers to buy the storied but troubled Dodge Brothers company. Dodge produced a full line of trucks and cars, such as this '30 Dodge Eight shown with Michigan athletic hero Bennie Osterbaan. (C)

Walter Chrysler completed purchase of Dodge Brothers on July 30, 1928, less than a week before the DeSoto introduction. At the heart of the deal were manufacturing facilities such as the huge, relatively integrated Dodge Main in Hamtramck, shown here, and a Graham truck-building plant in Evansville, Indiana. (C)

For DeSoto, Chrysler Corporation had to create an entirely new dealer organization, such as this modest showroom on Detroit's East Side. Earlier, Maxwell dealers had been happy to sign up for Chrysler, and the Dodge purchase brought the established Dodge car and Graham truck dealer network into the Chrysler fold. Two steps remained: changing Graham to Dodge Truck, and coupling Plymouth with all three senior brands, Chrysler, DeSoto, and Dodge. (C)

The spartan interior design of 1920s cars is apparent in this view inside a 1928 Plymouth coupe. Note the gearshift lever and parking brake mounted on the flat floor and the uncluttered instrument panel. (C)

Chrysler's strong new engine also found a ready market for powering boats like this ChrisCraft wooden-hulled speedboat. Marine engines required long-time full-throttle operation and few could stand up to the task as well as Chrysler's. (K)

In 1923, WPC purchased this Beaux-Arts mansion at Great Neck, Long Island, New York, after moving his family from their middle-class residence in Flint, Michigan. The 12-acre Chrysler estate became the home of the U.S. Merchant Marine Academy in 1942. Today the mansion serves as the Academy's administration building. (U)

Chrysler Corporation's sales successes were aided by memorable advertising. Two examples are shown on this page. Dodge Dependability was a theme played and replayed over many years, in this case to announce a 100,000-mile cross-country excursion by the new Dodge Eight in 1930. Dodge's all-steel body is credited in the ad copy for the car's durability. (C)

Chrysler promoted its engineering advances in advertisements such as this for Plymouth "floating power" engine mounting in 1931. At a time when car buyers were demanding increasing sophistication and comfort, floating power's promised freedom from vibration—especially for a 4-cylinder car—had great appeal. (C)

Less than three months after the 1929 stock market crash, the New York Auto Show opened in early 1930 with an incredible array of dashing automotive choices. Dodge and DeSoto both premiered new 8-cylinder models. Shown here is the Dodge display. Numerous makes introduced upscale and luxury models long in development. In 1929, its best year in the 1920s, Chrysler Corp. sold 367,000 cars for 9 percent of the U.S. market. (C)

New from Chrysler for 1931 were several more straight-8 engines and the classic Imperial, with custom bodies like this LeBaron Phaeton on a 145-inch wheelbase with a 385-cid engine. Seated right rear in this parade car, perhaps at the 1932 Presidential Inauguration, was New York Democratic leader Al Smith. Only 3,228 Imperials were sold in 1931 and the worst was yet to come. Yet Chrysler weathered the Depression better than most companies. (C)

Four

CONQUERING THE DEPRESSION

Completed in 1930, the Chrysler Building was the major—and the tallest—feature of the New York City skyline until surpassed by the Empire State Building a year later. The landmark was a personal project of Walter P. Chrysler, not Chrysler Corporation, though the company did keep offices there. It also symbolized the Kansas railroad mechanic's elevation to international prominence as both an auto baron and Manhattan magnate. The towering Art-Deco design appropriately closed out the runaway decade of the Roaring '20s, already crashing toward a deep economic depression—though at the time few paid heed to the warning signs of its very excesses. (C)

This rare photo of President Franklin D. Roosevelt with a withered, polio-paralyzed leg clearly visible as he sits behind the wheel of a hand-control-equipped 1933 DeSoto Cabriolet is one of the few showing his disability. Both he and his wife Eleanor drove and posed in Chrysler products. However, their '36 Ford touring car is displayed at the Roosevelt Library and Museum in Hyde Park, New York. (C)

In 1926, WPC hired one of his former Buick colleagues, K.T. Keller (1885–1966), as Chrysler Corp. vice president of manufacturing. Two years later, Chrysler put Keller in charge of Dodge. Here Keller is shown in his Dodge office with all the trappings of Roosevelt's New Deal—a portrait of FDR and a sign promoting the National Recovery Act. Keller succeeded WPC as president of Chrysler Corporation in 1935. (C)

After franchising Chrysler, DeSoto and Dodge dealers to sell Plymouths, WPC executed the next step in his strategy to increase sales: persuading potential buyers to consider Plymouth as well as market leaders Chevrolet and Ford, as illustrated here. "Look At All Three" with Chrysler himself—by now an authentic American hero—issuing the challenge was as famous in its day as Lee Iacocca's similar personal endorsements were 50 years later. (C)

By 1933, Plymouth's Four was no longer competitive with Chevrolet's Six and Ford's V-8. Chrysler responded by retiring the old Maxwell engine, replacing it with a 190-cid version of the original Chrysler Six, shown here. Plymouth sales increased 138,000 to 250,000 and Chrysler Corporation's 386,000 new car registrations made it number two in the industry for 1933 with a 26 percent market share, surpassing once mighty Ford. (C)

The One-Millionth Plymouth was built in 1934, a remarkable achievement in just six—mostly Depression—years. Here WPC is shown driving the milestone car from the final assembly line at the Lynch Road plant, opened in 1929 exclusively for Plymouth production. Its appearance shows none of the typical boxy lines from the earlier decade. (C)

One of WPC's proudest achievements was sponsoring the Chrysler Institute of Engineering which had its first graduation in 1933 (the 1946 ceremony is shown). The Institute offered a master's degree in automotive engineering, attracting graduates of the nation's most prestigious universities and providing a management pool for Chrysler and its competitors for decades. (C)

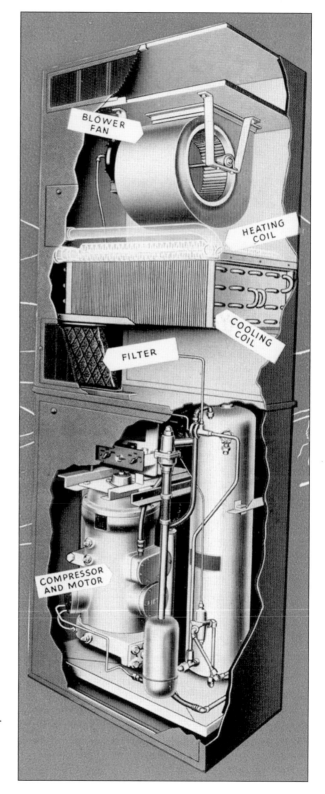

Chrysler Corporation's successful foray into air conditioning began with WPC's frustration about complaints from tenants in his new office building in New York City during a heat wave. Airtemp Division was formed in 1934 to develop and produce commercial units, such as shown here, and later introduced residential and eventually automotive applications. Chrysler sold Airtemp's name and commercial and residential business to raise needed cash after 1977. (C)

At the time of their 1934 introductions, WPC probably considered the advance design of the aerodynamic Airflow models the zenith of his contributions to the auto industry. Here he is shown proudly displaying a scale model of the radical vehicle, the first totally new design since conversion of the Maxwell-Chalmers lines to Chrysler ten years earlier. (C)

Airflows came in three different models: a long-wheelbase Imperial sedan plus Chrysler and DeSoto with two body styles each. All Chrysler Airflows were Eights and Chrysler energetically promoted their high-speed performance, as shown by the inscriptions on this sedan. But a public turned cautious by the Depression didn't take to the radical designs. (C)

Introduction of Airflow models was delayed many weeks by production problems which plagued the new cars. Chrysler and DeSoto sales for 1934 fell far below the year before in a rising market. Here Byron Foy, president of DeSoto and WPC's son-in-law, extolled virtues of a streamlined DeSoto Airflow Six coupe to a sophisticated crowd at the New York Auto Show. (C)

For 1935 Chrysler moved quickly to recover lost ground by offering conventional looking "Airstream" models to sell alongside Chrysler and DeSoto Airflows. In this ad, both Chrysler Airflow (left) and Airstream models are shown. DeSoto sold 6,800 Airflow models and 20,000 Airstreams in 1935, versus 14,000 Airflows the year before and 23,000 conventional DeSotos in 1933. (N)

This uncluttered instrument panel of '35 Plymouth shows another step in the progress of auto design. An advantage of the center-mounted instrument cluster was ready adaptability to both left-hand-drive conventional and RHD export models. Transmission and parking brake are still floor mounted and the starter plunger is seen clearly above the accelerator. Control for the single wiper is in the windshield header left of the mirror. (C)

Despite the setback from the Airflow, Chrysler Engineering continued with advanced design work, as illustrated by this Volkswagen-like small economy car shown under test in Northern Michigan in 1936. The experimental model, which never reached production, was powered by a radical 5-cylinder radial engine mounted for front-wheel-drive. (C)

A more practical short-term response to conditions in the mid-1930s was this '36 Plymouth developed for police forces in an era of bank robberies and other mobilized gangster activity. Note armor-plating to protect radiator and tires and the gun port in the windshield. (C)

Shown here is a familiar scene from the '30s, a delivery boy taking store wares directly to customers' homes in a car-based panel delivery truck like this '36 Dodge "camelback" model. Note also the tire chains on the rear wheels, the answer to slippery roads and deep snow before the development of snow tires. Chains were effective for traction but hard on tires and road surfaces. (C)

After the Airflow sales disaster of 1934–1935, DeSoto reverted to only conventional Airstream bodies while Chrysler continued with both through 1937. DeSoto also carved out a niche for itself as the preferred vehicle over Checker for city taxi service. Shown here is part of a massive driveway of '36 DeSoto taxis that were bound for New York. (C)

Already on the drawing boards when DeSoto sales crashed with the Airflow, Chrysler continued to build more production capacity by opening this DeSoto Plant at the far western edge of Detroit in 1936. The Albert Kahn-designed DeSoto factory was the only automobile assembly plant erected during the Depression. Chrysler erected a Dodge Truck plant in the northern suburb of Warren in 1938. (E)

In this picture, the Two Millionth Plymouth, a '37 (right), is lined up with the One Millionth of '34 and the first Plymouth of '28. Note the huge appearance change in ten years. As he had for the One Millionth, WPC drove the Two Millionth from the assembly line (cover). Chrysler announced that the California woman who bought the first Plymouth in '28 also took delivery of the milestone cars. (C)

The year 1937 marked significant auto industry economic recovery with U.S. deliveries of 3.5 million cars, up from a bottom of only 1.1 million in '32—despite lengthy "sit-down" strikes at GM, Chrysler and major suppliers by the United Auto Workers seeking to gain bargaining rights. Here victorious strikers, led by a marching band, emerge from Dodge Main in March 1937. (R)

With the growing popularity of car-based panel delivery and pickup light trucks, Chrysler provided its Chrysler-Plymouth and DeSoto-Plymouth dealer bodies with a commercial vehicle, the Plymouth truck, such as this '38. Basically, it was a Dodge truck with Plymouth front-end styling. Another spin-off from Dodge truck was the Fargo, sold in Canada and overseas. (C)

Unlike its traditional rivals, Chrysler avoided building overseas manufacturing facilities, relying instead on local distributor-assemblers to which it supplied export kits. Plymouths as such were not marketed overseas. They were re-badged and sold as lower-priced Chryslers in some countries, such as this custom-bodied Chrysler Wimbledon in the United Kingdom. To Americans. it looked like a '38 Plymouth. (D)

Headlights were mounted in the fenders of all Chrysler Corporation passenger cars, like this Plymouth, for the 1939 Model Year. This was also the last year Chrysler offered a convertible four-door sedan. Twenty years before, 90 percent of the industry's output had been for open cars. Just 387 of these Plymouths were built, making them highly desirable for 21st-century collectors. (D)

Also for '39, Plymouth was selected by Chrysler to introduce an industry first—the power top for convertible coupes illustrated here. The power top was actuated by vacuum power created by the stroking of engine pistons. Vacuum power also was used for windshield wipers. Wheelbase was 114 inches for '39 Plymouths, except for the 117-in convertible sedan. (C)

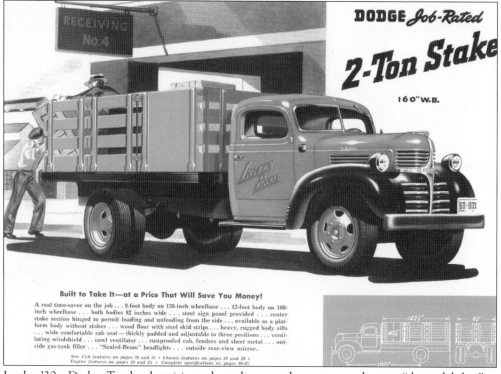

In the '30s, Dodge Truck advertising adopted a new theme to supplement "dependability"—Job-Rated, as shown in this pitch for the '41 2-Ton model. Such a truck was a descendant of the earlier Graham line, being based on unique heavy-duty components rather than just modified passenger car parts like the Dodge and Plymouth pickup and panel delivery trucks. (C)

Celebrated as the Four-Millionth Plymouth, this stylish '41 convertible also illustrated the last of external running boards on American cars. Widening bodies to conceal running boards provided wider front and rear seats, and made cars comfortable for six passengers. Chrysler maintained its second place position in the auto industry, held since 1936, with sales of 902,000 and a 24 percent market share for 1941. (C)

This photo of a '41 Dodge business coupe, marketed to traveling salesmen who didn't need a rear passenger seat but valued the huge trunk, illustrates one of Chrysler's safety features—the separate, trunk-mounted brake light. Chrysler's '41 models also introduced safety-rim wheels, a flange which deterred tire separation from blowouts. (D)

From 1941 through 1948, Chrysler's cars all presented instrument layouts similar to the '41 Chrysler panel shown. "Fluid Drive" was Chrysler's semi-automatic transmission, introduced late in '39 as an Imperial option. Unlike GM's HydraMatic, a clutch was still needed to shift into forward or reverse. From '39 through '42, the "safety speedometer" changed colors from green to yellow to red to warn the driver as speed increased. (C)

This sleek Chrysler Newport phaeton was one of a pair of futuristic "dream cars" unveiled by Chrysler in 1941. A companion was the two-door Thunderbolt with disappearing steel top. Six Newports were built—initially for an Indianapolis 500 Race pace car, later for display at shows, fairs, and dealerships. This survivor can be viewed at Chrysler's Auburn Hills, Michigan, museum and at collector car shows. (D)

The auto industry's 1942 Model Year was aborted by the attack on Pearl Harbor on December 7, 1941. Civilian car production ended by February 2, 1942, and civilian truck production a month later. The '42 DeSoto shown marked Chrysler's one-model-year trial of disappearing headlights. Two-door sedans were the industry's most popular pre-war body style, valued by families with children who feared they might fall from open rear doors. (C)

Five

WINNING THE WAR AND POST-WAR RECOVERY

Awakened from peacetime complacency by war starting in Europe in 1939, America and its industry responded by tooling up for military vehicle production. Chrysler won a contract to mass-produce tanks, such as these M-3s, beginning in 1941 at a new tank plant erected near the Dodge Truck plant and the U.S. Army Tank and Automotive Command in Warren, Michigan. Chrysler built 22,235 tanks during World War II and became America's prime tank-developer and builder throughout the Cold War. Indeed, Chrysler arguably was the world's largest tank builder during the 20th century—certainly in the non-Communist part of the world. (C)

In this rare photo taken in the early days of World War II, the presidents of the Big Three auto manufacturers confer, something they would not have been allowed to do in peacetime because of government anti-trust fears. From left to right are K.T. Keller of Chrysler, Charles E. Wilson of General Motors, and Edsel Ford of Ford Motor. In 1940, William S. Knudsen, Wilson's predecessor at GM, had resigned to become chief of American defense production. (C)

One of Chrysler Corporation's lasting contributions to motoring history was the four-wheel-drive Dodge Command Car built for Army use. It was derived from Dodge pickup trucks and was an ancestor of today's Sport Utility Vehicles. Early Command Car versions like this retained civilian Dodge Truck identity, while later versions were anonymously "GI" ("government-issue") with utilitarian flat sheet metal. Chrysler produced nearly 400,000 trucks and truck-based ambulances for the war effort. (C)

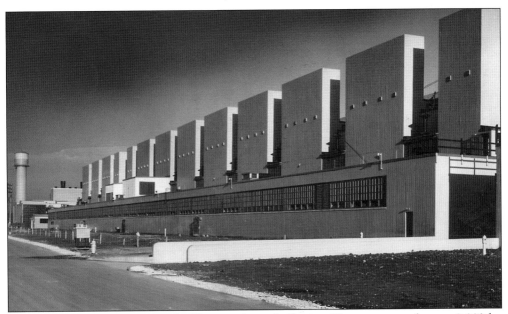

Chrysler erected the mammoth Chicago Aircraft Engine Plant to manufacture 2,000-hp Wright engines for the B-29 Superfortress bomber. Construction began in May 1942, but it was 1944 before engines were produced for the long-range bombers to attack Japanese home islands. After the war the plant was leased from the government by Preston Tucker for assembly of his ill-fated car, of which only 50 were made. (C)

Operation of the Chicago Aircraft Engine Plant was assigned to Dodge Division, and L.L. (Tex) Colbert was named manager. Here, late in the war, Colbert (left) poses with Boeing Aircraft and Army Air Force personnel in front of a Boeing-assembled B-29 bomber powered by one of the engines built at his plant. (C)

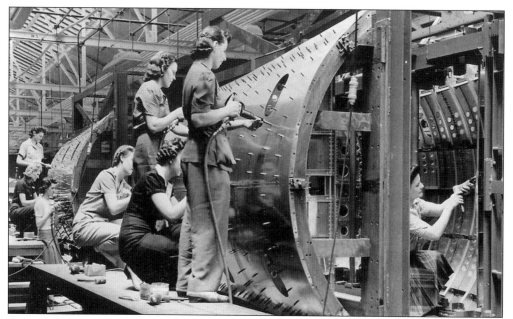

One of World War II's enduring images was "Rosie the Riveter," the prototypical housewife turned war worker for the West Coast's aircraft industry. But Chrysler had its own Rosies, as shown by this photo of female employees at the DeSoto plant in Detroit, producing fuselage sections for Martin B-26 medium bombers. Nearly 1,600 such aircraft body sections were turned out at DeSoto by war's end. (C)

During the war, the Allies' most reliable and widely used armored fighting vehicle was the M-4 Sherman tank, which replaced the earlier M-3 in Chrysler Tank Plant production even before Pearl Harbor. Here a battalion of U.S. 5th Army Sherman tanks lines up for an attack on German positions near Pistraloma, Italy, in October 1944. (C-U.S. Army Signal Corps photograph)

By chance, one of Chrysler's most important contributions to Allied victory was a choice by atomic energy scientists at Los Alamos, New Mexico, to carry the plutonium heart of the first atomic bomb from the laboratory some 330 miles to the Alamogordo test site in the back seat of a 1942 Plymouth Army staff car. Here the scientists lift the device from the car the day before the atomic age dawned. (S)

With the war over late in 1945, hundreds of thousands of American service men and women began returning home from overseas. One of the most revered returning soldiers was General Dwight D. Eisenhower, Allied commander in Europe. Here he is shown in a post-war motorcade through New York's Central Park, riding in a '40 Chrysler parade limousine. (C)

At war's end, there was a pent-up worldwide demand for new vehicles to supply units destroyed, worn out, or utilized by the military. Chrysler was late among Detroit automakers to restart civilian production at plants like East Jefferson Assembly, shown here. It was bordered to the east (left) by the Hudson plant. (C)

To meet the post-war demand, Chrysler and other automakers converted war production plants and built new facilities. Among these was a Dodge plant at San Leandro, California, where K.T. Keller is shown inspecting initial output of new Dodge trucks and passenger cars. Chrysler's first post-war cars were essentially minor facelifts from the 1942 models. (C)

Chrysler first introduced its wood-and-steel-bodied Town & Country models with a '41 "beetleback" station wagon. After the war, with the added incentive of a steel shortage, both sedan and convertible wood-bodied models like this '47 were offered. All T&Cs were top-of-the-line models, powered by the 8-cylinder L-head engines first used in 1930. (C)

Just as General Motors had designed its "no-vent" wing windows to cater to smokers in the 1930s, DeSoto offered an optional package for '42 and '46 models that included this cigarette dispenser built into the steering wheel hub. To meet public demand in a different age, throughout the auto industry all cars provided ash trays and electric cigarette lighters were standard in upper series models, optional in all. (C)

The production custom body business which figured so prominently in the creation of classic cars in the late-'20s and early-'30s (p. 36) was on its last legs by the late-'40s. Here is a Derham-bodied limousine built on a '47 Chrysler Imperial chassis. Its squarish lines from an earlier era seem incompatible with the Chrysler's rounded sheet metal. (N)

DeSoto continued its large volume taxi and commercial limousine sales in the late Forties, almost entirely on long-wheelbase (139.5-in vs. 121.5) bodies, also offered by Chrysler and Dodge. DeSoto's Suburban limousine body permitted rear seating for as many as six and was popular for transportation at resorts such as this Arkansas spa. DeSoto's 1946-7-8 production (when there were no design changes) totaled 253,000. (N)

Six

CHALLENGE, STUMBLE, AND COMEBACK

In 1950, after 15 years that arguably were Chrysler's most successful in terms of market share, profits, and reputation, K.T. Keller relinquished the presidency of the company. His influence was total after WPC's death in 1940, and extended into the mid-1950s in terms of product design. Keller and engineering chief Fred Zeder steadfastly believed cars should be practical and comfortable with chair height seats, wide-opening doors, and roofs high enough in which to wear a hat. Unfortunately for Chrysler, the public became more enthralled with the "longer, lower, wider" products offered by cutthroat competitors. Keller is shown here shortly before his retirement with a model of one of his ideal, but "boxy," cars. (C)

For 1949, Chrysler presented all-new bodies for the first time since 1940. Plymouth and Dodge came in two separate wheelbases. This Plymouth Special Deluxe "woody" wagon on a 118.5-in wheelbase was nearly the last of its type. Long-wheelbase Plymouths also included a two-door club coupe, a four-door sedan and a convertible. (N)

This 111-in wheelbase all-steel Plymouth Suburban wagon, priced at $1,840, quickly eclipsed the longer woody above, with production of 19,220 against only 3,443 for the other. Suburbans paved the way for competitors' station wagons to have all steel bodies in subsequent years. (N)

The stubby short-wheelbase '49 Plymouth and a Dodge business coupe were the last of the unique blind-quarter body type in the industry. This Plymouth also became the car to beat on NASCAR racetracks because of its favorable power-to-weight ratio. A third short-wheelbase Plymouth was a fastback two-door sedan. (N)

The most unusual of
the '49 models was
this Dodge Wayfarer
roadster on a
115-inch wheelbase. A
throwback to the early
'30s, it was a
front-seat-only
convertible with
neither power top
nor roll-down side
windows. Longer
123.5-in wheelbase
Dodges sold better. (N)

The '49 Chrysler's
interior had a
swept-away instrument
panel, safety padded
dash and the
chair-height seats
common to all the
company's new cars
that year. Note the
instrument cluster in
front of the steering
wheel and the parking
brake handle to the left
of the wheel. (N)

This artwork from
a Dodge sales
brochure illustrates
one of Chrysler's
most lasting
innovations for
'49—ignition-key
starting. All the
company's '49s also
offered electric
windshield wipers
and automatic
chokes. (C)

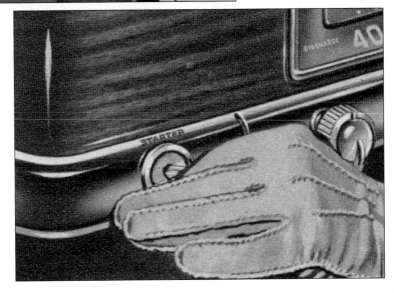

L.L. (Tex) Colbert (1905–1995) was a Texan with a Harvard Law degree. With Keller as his mentor, he was brought into Dodge management in the 1930s. After heading the wartime Aircraft Engine Plant (p. 55), he became president of Dodge, which became the traditional route to the top at Chrysler. He succeeded Keller as president of Chrysler Corporation on November 3, 1950, with KT staying on as board chairman until 1966. (C)

Despite such promotional efforts as calendar girls posing with new '50 Chrysler hardtop models, Chrysler suffered mightily during Keller's last active year. A successful pension-seeking 104-day UAW strike disrupted production and Chrysler lost its second place in industry sales, never to regain it, to a reborn Ford Motor Company. (C)

New Chrysler products for the 1951 Model Year included this handsome Imperial with separate front-and-rear styling from other Chryslers for the first time in nearly 20 years. The Korean War broke out in June 1950, only a few weeks before production of '51 models was to begin, but did not affect the auto business until the following year. (N)

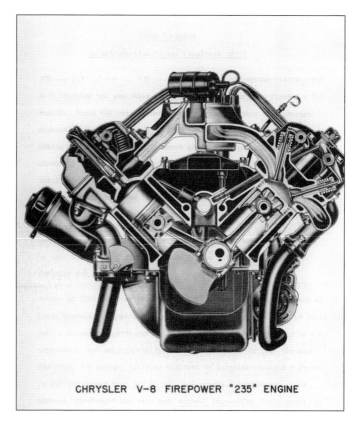

CHRYSLER V-8 FIREPOWER "235" ENGINE

Chrysler's major innovation for 1951 was this 331-cid, 180-hp engine. It was the first V-8 in Chrysler history and the company's first all-new engine design since the original Six of 1924. It was dubbed "Hemi" from the hemispherical shape of the combustion chambers. The Hemi was a competitive response to GM and began an industry horsepower race. Another 1951 Chrysler innovation was power steering. (C)

Carrera Panamericana (Mexican Road Race), a major motor sports event of the early-'50s, was an all-out 1,900-mile race across Mexico between Texas and Guatemala. In 1950, its first year, the event was won by an Olds 88. For '51 the "winner" was a Chrysler Saratoga with the new Hemi engine. Two Ferrari factory race cars finished ahead of the Saratoga, but they were scarcely mass-production family cars like this 2-ton $3,000 Chrysler. (P)

As the post-war sellers' market receded in the early-'50s, Chrysler brought forth a wave of dream cars designed by Virgil Exner and executed by Italian coachbuilder Ghia. Here a crowd crushes around the K-310 displayed in the Chrysler factory showroom on East Jefferson. K-310 design elements such as the deck lid, tail lights, and grille showed up on later Chrysler production cars. (C)

In mid-1952, DeSoto got its version of the Hemi V-8, called the Firedome, at 276-cid and 160-hp slightly tamer than the Chrysler engine. This shows the 1953 DeSoto front end with the trademark toothy "waterfall" grille, featured since 1941, and a new "Vee" on the hood to signify the engine type. It was the first Eight for DeSoto since 1932. (N)

After World War II, Chrysler expanded its export offerings by adding a DeSoto-badged Plymouth called the DeSoto Diplomat, shown here as a 1951 right-hand-drive model for Australia. The DeSoto nameplate also played well in Spanish-speaking markets, especially Mexico. Later Australian Chrysler products were unique from American models, although they used many common components and design cues. (N)

DEPENDABILITY THROUGH THE YEARS

Model Year 1953 brought the last of the conservative Keller/Zeder car designs, with all-new bodies for a 114-in wheelbase Plymouth and 119-in Dodge, the latter shown here amidst an array of previous Dodges. Although Chrysler never seems to have used the slogan, press accounts praised the company's junior '53 cars as "smaller on the outside, bigger on the inside." This year Dodge also got its own Hemi V-8, signified by a Vee on the hood like Imperial, Chrysler, and DeSoto V-8s. The company finally introduced its first clutchless automatic, dubbed Powerflite, late in the model year for Imperial and Chrysler. Total Chrysler U.S. new car registrations rose in a growing market to a record 1,165,000, including 154,000 Chryslers and Imperials, 122,000 DeSotos, 289,000 Dodges, and 600,000 Plymouths. But share continued to slide, down to 20 percent from a high of 26 percent in 1946. (N)

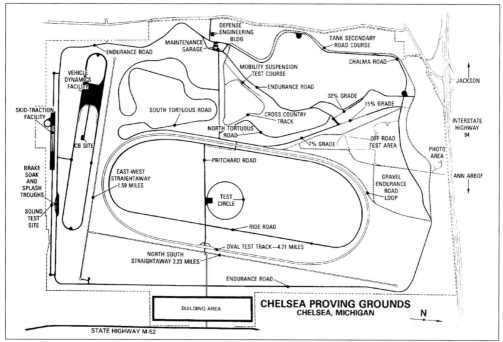

The following year, 1954, resulted in a roller coaster of good and bad news for Chrysler. Heading the good news was the opening of Chrysler's first proving ground—with the huge variety of facilities and roadways shown by this map—near Chelsea, Michigan. GM, Ford, and Packard had developed such facilities many years before. (C)

Chrysler rounded up these Plymouth taxicabs from all over the country for the new test track's press preview to testify to the car's practicality. Plymouths were popular with police, too, because the high seats were easier on backs during long patrol shifts. Sales competition between GM and Ford in 1954 proved disastrous for Chrysler and the independents. Chrysler's sales dropped 37 percent and market share fell to 13 percent, lowest since 1931. (C)

In what was a recession year for Chrysler, the company nevertheless continued its custom of supplying parade cars for New York City (pp. 36 and 57) and other ceremonial occasions with this custom Ghia-built '54 Imperial dual-cowl phaeton. The sign indicates it was being prepped for use as the official car for President Eisenhower's "Garrison Dam Closure Ceremonies." (C)

This Norseman (supposedly to be promoted as a DeSoto) was the dream car that became a nightmare. It was conceived by Exner, built by Ghia, and was on its way to U.S. auto shows in the S.S. Andria Doria's cargo hull when the Italian luxury liner collided with a freighter off the coast of Long Island and sank. The Norseman rests on the bottom of the Atlantic, but its fastback design survived on the '66 Dodge Charger (p. 91). (C)

Late in 1954, Chrysler moved to integrate its manufacturing base by buying Briggs Manufacturing which made bodies for Plymouth. Here the Briggs' sign is being changed. Unfortunately the purchase cut off body supplies to Hudson and Packard, helping force them into mergers with Nash and Studebaker, respectively, and the two vintage Detroit nameplates soon disappeared. (C)

By the mid-'50s, Plymouth was a separate division within Chrysler, headquartered here at the Lynch Road plant on Detroit's northeast side. In mid-1954 the plant was busily tooling for its second major body change in just two years. The "Forward Look" of 1955 was the Colbert/Exner effort to reverse Chrysler's fortunes in a highly competitive car market. (C)

This two-tone green '55 Plymouth Savoy Club Sedan was my first new car. Plymouth's version of the Forward Look presented the cleanest appearance of any Chrysler products that year. It was also Plymouth's first year for a V8, which I selected, and fully automatic transmission, which I scorned. With this 115-in wheelbase model, Plymouth made a comeback in sales—but not enough to regain the third place it had given up to Buick in 1954. (D)

For '55, Chrysler introduced its high-performance 300 coupe, shown here racing on the famous—and now long-abandoned—beach-and-road course of the Daytona 500. The Forward Look brought a 69 percent sales gain and profitability for the number three automaker but market share increased only modestly, to 17 percent, in the auto industry's booming 7.2-million car sales year. (C)

Lined up for a corporate advertisement, all of Chrysler's '56 models are pictured here: Imperial and Chrysler (rear), DeSoto (center), and Dodge and Plymouth (front). Use of the USAF jet fighter emphasized the company's advanced styling. Chrysler's financial position was stressed again by tooling costs for a major design change for 1957, the third cycle in just five years—after the stability of only two cycles from '40 to '52. (C)

In 1956, mindlessly inviting criticism from government and intellectual circles, the auto industry surged into the triple sales extravagances of styling excesses, horsepower races, and race sponsorships. Plymouth's entry was the souped-up Fury model, shown here in the foreground among other "stock" race cars at Michigan's Flat Rock track. Led by Ford, safety options like seat belts were introduced—but the public couldn't have cared less. (C)

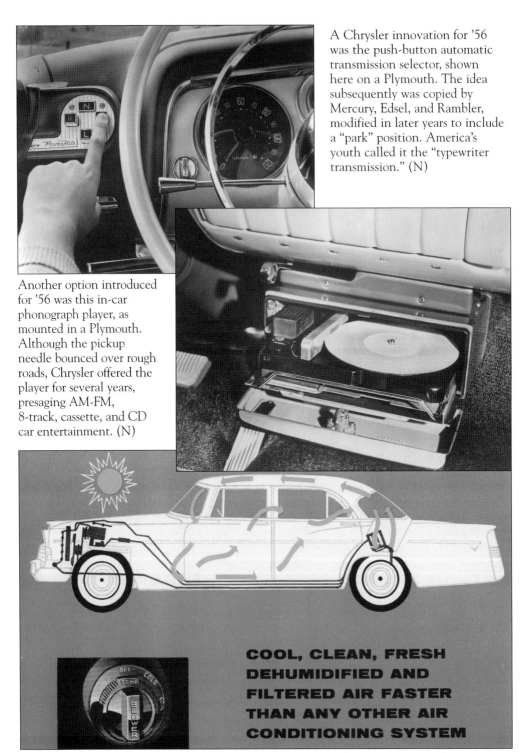

A Chrysler innovation for '56 was the push-button automatic transmission selector, shown here on a Plymouth. The idea subsequently was copied by Mercury, Edsel, and Rambler, modified in later years to include a "park" position. America's youth called it the "typewriter transmission." (N)

Another option introduced for '56 was this in-car phonograph player, as mounted in a Plymouth. Although the pickup needle bounced over rough roads, Chrysler offered the player for several years, presaging AM-FM, 8-track, cassette, and CD car entertainment. (N)

COOL, CLEAN, FRESH DEHUMIDIFIED AND FILTERED AIR FASTER THAN ANY OTHER AIR CONDITIONING SYSTEM

Chrysler drew on its Airtemp commercial and residential air conditioning expertise for automotive creature comfort. This 1956 sales brochure illustration shows the rear mounting which preceded A/C units hung under the dash (p. 81) or integrated into instrument panels in later years. (C)

Chrysler spent $300 million on its all-new '57s—a huge amount for the time—like this 122-in wheelbase Dodge Custom Royal Lancer, 5 inches lower than previous models. Plymouth's wheelbase increased to 118 in. Chrysler didn't invent tailfins, but made the most of them in 1957. Total company car sales were nearly 1.1 million and market share rose to 18 percent, the highest since 1953. Plymouth regained third place in sales. (N)

NEW TORSION BARS. When Plymouth travels over rough roads, powerful torsion bars twist, and thus absorb bumps before they can reach the car's frame. Keeps your car riding smooth and level.

By 1957, station wagons like this Dodge (left) had replaced two-door sedans as the family car. Chrysler's new wagons, all on 122-in wheelbases, featured the rear-facing third seat, a widely copied design. (N) Chrysler also introduced a radical new front-suspension—torsion-bars in place of coil springs —in its '57s, as illustrated (right) in this Plymouth brochure. This concept, unlike the rear-facing seat, was not copied. (C)

In 1958, recognizing the growing popularity in North America of imported economy cars such as Volkswagen, Renault, European Fords, and Opels and Vauxhalls from GM, Chrysler purchased a minority ownership in the French Simca Company. It began importing cars like these to the American market while obtaining a manufacturing toehold in Europe. Imports captured 10 percent of the 1959 U.S. car market. (C)

Britain's Queen Elizabeth II and Prince Phillip are shown riding in a custom '59 Crown Imperial during their tour of Canada. Only seven Crowns were built that year, all on a 149.5-in wheelbase. Such royal attention was a highlight for Chrysler and the industry after an otherwise dismal recession year in 1958, when industry sales fell to 4.2 million. In 1959, Chrysler's share plunged to only 11 percent, the worst since 1930. (C)

Seven

PROLIFERATION

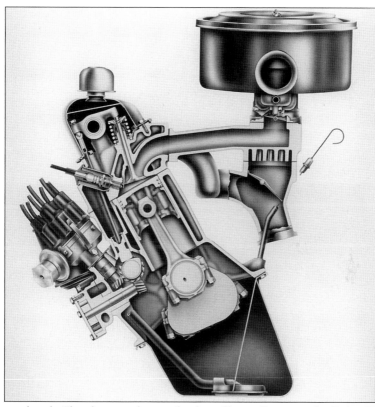

The '60s opened with Chrysler introducing the first all-new Six since the Zeder-Skelton-Breer L-head engine of 1924. This radical over-head-valve "Slant Six" fitted under the lower hood lines now in vogue and was offered in two sizes: 170-cid for the new Valiant and 225-cid for standard-sized Plymouth and Dodge. Countering the import invasion, the Big Three introduced the small, so-called compact cars they had been considering since the 1930s (p. 44). The 106.5-in wheelbase Valiant offered many unique features and fitted neatly between Ford's conservative Falcon and Chevrolet's radical rear-engined Corvair. The new-sized cars also opened the door to a proliferation of models in the '60s, each requiring costly design, tooling and marketing expenditures. The additions were supported to some extent by an expanding overall market of prosperity and "two-car families." (C)

The decade also began with an unexpected upheaval in Chrysler management. W.C. Newberg (left), Chrysler Institute graduate and head of Dodge since 1950, became president in April 1960, succeeding Tex Colbert (right), who advanced to chairman of the board in the established Chrysler pattern. But only two months later, Newberg resigned amidst conflict-of-interest charges. Colbert soldiered on under heavy criticism from disgruntled stockholders until retiring in mid-1961. (N)

This new team then took over Chrysler. In a 1967 photo are, left to right, Lynn A. Townsend, George H. Love, and Virgil E. Boyd. An accountant before joining Chrysler in 1957, Townsend (1919–2000) served as president 1961–1966 and chairman, 1967–1975. Love, a mining company executive and outside director, was chairman 1961–66. Boyd (1912–), a GM and Nash veteran, was hired from American Motors in 1962 to rejuvenate sales and was president 1967–1970. (C)

When the new Valiant was unveiled to automotive editors in the fall of 1959, it received an unprecedented standing ovation for its sassy looks. In addition to the Slant Six, it offered a floor-mounted manual transmission and alternator in place of the conventional DC generator. Here the author, then a reporter for Business Week magazine, posed while test-driving Valiants at the Chelsea Proving Ground. (D)

The two-passenger XNR sports roadster with its single, off-center "boattail," was a spin-off from Valiant, unveiled in March 1960. It was one of Virgil Exner's last dream cars and was named after him. Here it is being loaded into a highway tractor-trailer van for shipment to auto shows around the country. (C)

The new decade marked the beginning of a new distribution system for Chrysler, shown by these two distinct '60 Dodge models, a 118-in wheelbase Plymouth-sized Dart (left) and a fully medium-price competitor, the Polara with a 122-in base. Each had distinctive—and costly to tool—rear quarter panels, trim, and grille. The next step was separation of the Plymouth franchise from Dodge dealers. (C)

Chrysler also introduced new bodies for 1960 after only a three-year cycle. The new "unibodies" featured a construction in which reinforced body metal panels were welded together without the separate body being bolted to a frame. The welded bodies were treated to "sheep dips"— complete immersion paint priming, as shown here at the Plymouth Lynch Road Plant—for critical protection against corrosion from road salt. (C)

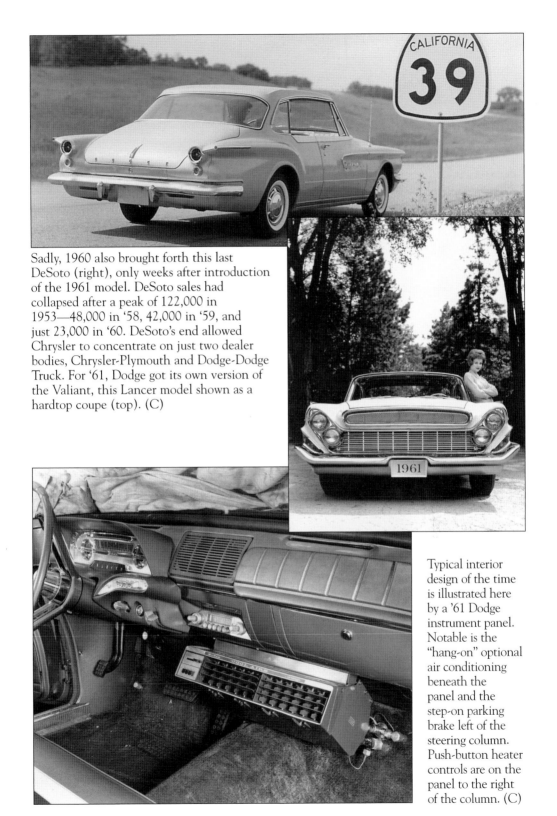

Sadly, 1960 also brought forth this last DeSoto (right), only weeks after introduction of the 1961 model. DeSoto sales had collapsed after a peak of 122,000 in 1953—48,000 in '58, 42,000 in '59, and just 23,000 in '60. DeSoto's end allowed Chrysler to concentrate on just two dealer bodies, Chrysler-Plymouth and Dodge-Dodge Truck. For '61, Dodge got its own version of the Valiant, this Lancer model shown as a hardtop coupe (top). (C)

Typical interior design of the time is illustrated here by a '61 Dodge instrument panel. Notable is the "hang-on" optional air conditioning beneath the panel and the step-on parking brake left of the steering column. Push-button heater controls are on the panel to the right of the column. (C)

After recovering with its '60 models, Chrysler again misjudged the market for '62 when, after just a two-year cycle, it brought out "sawed off" shorter car bodies such as this 116-in wheelbase Dodge Dart. While the industry soared more than a million units higher in 1962, Chrysler gained only 35,000 and its share dropped to under 10 percent. Plymouth, with sales down one-third in two years, fell to 7th place. (C)

A public relations bonus for Chrysler came in 1962 when Mamie Eisenhower, former First Lady, took delivery of a new Valiant. A Chrysler representative points out features to Mrs. Eisenhower as former President Eisenhower looks on at their Pennsylvania home. Note the personalized front license plate. (C)

Thanks to its years of negotiating and filling military contracts, Chrysler was well positioned to be successful bidder for two unique—for Detroit—Federal government contracts in the early 1960s. The first was to supply the massive, movable waiting rooms for Dulles International Airport in Virginia, where President John F. Kennedy is shown on an inspection in 1961. These unusual "people movers" are still in service 40 years later. (C)

The second massive government contract held by Chrysler for many years, beginning in the '50s, involved development and construction of Redstone, Jupiter (scale models shown here at an exhibition), and Saturn rockets for military purposes and the U.S. Space program. (C)

In 1962 Chrysler embarked on a massive "consumer evaluation" of gas-turbine-powered cars. Some 200 motorists across the country were carefully chosen for three-month "tests" of the 50 Turbine Cars built. Here mechanics are shown readying a turbine "power pack" for installation in one of the Ghia bodies. But engineers could not solve inherent fuel economy problems with turbines, which never reached mass production for motor vehicles—at Chrysler or elsewhere. (C)

After the Chevrolet Corvair Monza had demonstrated that the public wanted sporty compact cars as well as plain economy sedans, Ford and Chrysler swung into place—for example, this '63 Plymouth Valiant convertible. Also for '63, Dodge switched names: the compact Lancer became a Dart and the standard-sized Dart became a Polara. To counter adverse buyer reaction to "downsized" '62s, most '63s from Chrysler were slightly longer. (C)

Dodge's new family of Valiant-based "compact trucks" reached the market in 1963, more than two years after Ford and Chevrolet had introduced such models. Of these small Dodge haulers, all mounted on short 90-inch wheelbases, the pickup version failed to survive, as was the case with competitive compact pickups of the time. The minibus carried nine passengers. (C)

A new fad of the '60s was the growing interest in camping out. Dodge issued this press release photo demonstrating after-market camper equipment mounted atop a compact '63 Dart sedan (left) and a full-sized Dodge wagon. Later in the decade, pickup truck beds became more popular as platforms for such campers. (C)

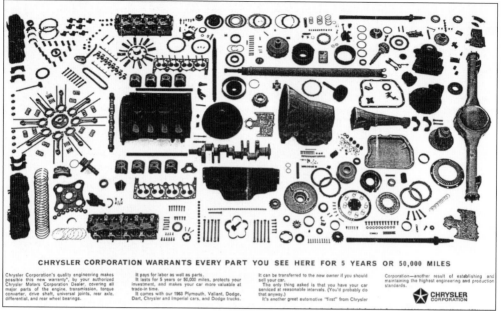

CHRYSLER CORPORATION WARRANTS EVERY PART YOU SEE HERE FOR 5 YEARS OR 50,000 MILES

Chrysler Corporation's quality engineering makes possible this new warranty", by your authorized Chrysler Motors Corporation Dealer, covering all major parts of the engine, transmission, torque converter, drive shaft, universal joints, rear axle, differential, and rear wheel bearings.

It pays for labor as well as parts. It lasts for 5 years or 50,000 miles, protects your investment, and makes your car more valuable at trade-in time. It comes with our 1963 Plymouth, Valiant, Dodge, Dart, Chrysler and Imperial cars, and Dodge trucks.

It can be transferred to the new owner if you should sell your car. The only thing asked is that you have your car serviced at reasonable intervals. (You'd probably do that anyway.) It's another great automotive "first" from Chrysler

Corporation—another result of establishing and maintaining the highest engineering and production standards.

CHRYSLER CORPORATION

Late in 1962, Chrysler announced that its 1963 models would carry a "5/50" powertrain warranty— good for 5 years or 50,000 miles, whichever came first. This was the final escalation in a "warranty war" Ford had kicked off with a 12-month/12,000-mile warranty for '61s except Lincoln, which got 24/24. This Chrysler corporate ad dramatically illustrated all the powertrain parts covered. (C)

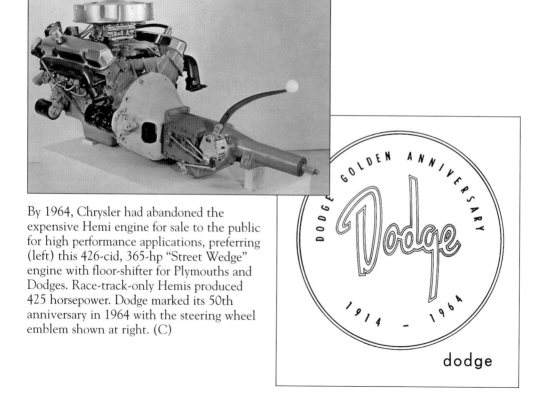

By 1964, Chrysler had abandoned the expensive Hemi engine for sale to the public for high performance applications, preferring (left) this 426-cid, 365-hp "Street Wedge" engine with floor-shifter for Plymouths and Dodges. Race-track-only Hemis produced 425 horsepower. Dodge marked its 50th anniversary in 1964 with the steering wheel emblem shown at right. (C)

DODGE GOLDEN ANNIVERSARY
Dodge
1914 - 1964

dodge

86

By 1964, Chrysler's strategies—5/50 warranty, larger cars, better styling, aggressive marketing of high performance—were paying off. The company's 1964 car sales exceeded a million for the first time since 1957. Market share was gaining a percentage point a year in a rising market. Here at Dodge Main, a wagon is assembled at the traditional body drop. (C)

On November 14, 1964, Dodge Main surpassed all previous annual production records when its 421,302nd car, this '65 Dart GT hardtop, was assembled. Dodge Main thus became the first assembly plant in the industry in '64 to exceed its prior-year production. At right is John J. Riccardo (1924–), then assistant general manager of Dodge— later president (1970–1975) and chairman (1975–1979) of Chrysler. (C)

Chrysler tried to distract from Ford's Mustang introduction in April 1964 by rushing out its own "pony car"—this Valiant-based Barracuda—two weeks earlier. Barracuda remained an important part of Plymouth's offerings through 1974. (C)

For the 1965 Model Year, Plymouth brought back the full-sized car it had abandoned in 1962. This provided Plymouth with cars in three distinct sizes: compact (Valiant/Barracuda), intermediate (Belvedere/Satellite), and the full-sized Fury, shown here in the station wagon version. (C)

Chrysler's practice of supplying custom Ghia-built Crown Imperial limousines ended in 1965 with only ten built. Two of the three sold in America were photographed here at a 1978 car collector meeting in Windsor, Ontario. One had been owned by the widow of Dodge founder Horace Dodge and the other by the Quebec government. (C)

To compete in a rapidly growing mid-sized "muscle car" market in North America, for 1966 Dodge introduced the fastbacked Charger shown here. Most auto historians credit Pontiac with identifying and exploiting the market in 1964 with its big-engined GTO coupe. Dodge Charger's 1966 production of 37,300 exceeded the GTO's first year of 32,500. (C)

Once again flush with profits from its mid-'60s comeback in the American market, Chrysler unwisely invested in the Rootes Motors Group of Britain, an amalgamation of several vehicle companies with inefficient production facilities and troubled work forces. Even having this Sunbeam Alpine roadster in the product line-up ultimately failed to produce either success in the United Kingdom market or viable exports to America. (N)

Chrysler expanded its inboard boat engine business (p. 34), dating from the 1920s, into a full-fledged Marine Division, purchasing outboard engine and boat-hull manufacturers. A full line of personal watercraft was offered, ranging from row-boats to speedboats (shown here) and cabin cruisers to sailboats. The company opened a new facility at Marine City, Michigan, for the business. (A)

In the late 1960s, Chrysler greatly expanded its real estate operations. Starting from simple help for auto dealers to obtain better facilities and manage Chrysler's own facilities, the operation soon entered commercial real estate investment and management. Among the developments were office parks, resort properties, upscale residential areas, and shopping malls like this one in Las Vegas, Nevada. (A)

The new-bodied 108-in wheelbase Valiant sedans introduced for 1967 were to have a relatively long model run. The conservative, pleasantly-styled four-door would last through the 1976 model year with only minor changes as Plymouth's basic bread-and-butter car. The spin-off sporty Barracuda offered fastback, notchback, and convertible models in 1967. From '65 through '68 Plymouth regained fourth place, behind Pontiac. (C)

Chrysler President Virgil Boyd posed here with a '68 Chrysler New Yorker. He helped shepherd the corporation through a string of profitable years in which market share remained steadily in the 15–16 percent range while the industry enjoyed record sales volumes. Chrysler new car registrations exceeded 200,000 annually from 1965 through 1969, and the corporation, more than a million a year for 11 years after 1963. (C)

During this period, Chrysler specialized in bargain-basement muscle cars like the Plymouth Road Runner, the name based on a popular TV cartoon character shown on the car's logo decal (top). Dodge's companion car was the Super Bee, pictured here (center) at an auto show display. Both models were built on mid-sized platforms with big V-8s. Chrysler products paved a blaze of glory all during the '60s and '70s on racetracks and drag strips. Plymouth's number-one driver, Richard Petty, is shown (bottom) racing at a NASCAR oval track in his famed Number 43, here a '68 Plymouth Road Runner. (C)

Eight

OVER-EXPANSION AND RETRACTION

The '70s opened on a high note for Chrysler with market share of 16 percent—1,350,000 registered car sales in an 8.4-million year. The industry had weathered the Vietnam War without so much as a blink—it simply wasn't involved. But there were warning signs of growing consumer backlash against Detroit, measured in first-ever Federal regulation of vehicle safety and air pollution standards and threatened damage-resistance requirements. Most of all, the public was beginning to reject Detroit's and Chrysler's staple—the big V-8. Imported cars jumped more than three points to gain 15 percent of the 1970 market, mostly from GM. Chrysler made one of the smartest moves in its history when in 1970 it began importing the Dodge-badged Colt shown here on a Los Angeles dock and later bought an interest in Japan's Mitsubishi. The relationship was to extend, in one form or another, into the 21st century. (N)

What was thought to be the "last" Chrysler convertible was the 122-in wheelbase '70 Newport model at the rear in this publicity shot. It was also the last year for full-sized Plymouth and Dodge convertibles. Chrysler brand sales at the 150-160,000 level in the early 1970s represented a significant decline from the 200,000-plus volumes of the late-'60s. (C)

The Valiant-based Plymouth Duster coupe, introduced for 1970, became Chrysler's runaway sales champ, selling well over 200,000 units annually for the next five years as the company's low-priced domestic entry. The "340" model pictured boasted a large V-8 rather than the economical Slant Six. (C)

One of the most unusual-looking American cars ever was this '70 Plymouth Superbird with elongated "snout" and "flying wing" rear spoiler to improve high-speed aerodynamics. Based on the mid-sized Road Runner, a handful—1,920—were built in order to comply with NASCAR regulations, but basically the Superbird was just a race car. Here Richard Petty hurls his Superbird around a speedway somewhere in the Southeast early in 1971. (C)

1971 was a banner year for Petty, Plymouth's long-time main contract NASCAR driver. He not only won the NASCAR championship for the third consecutive year, but here he and his '71 Plymouth Number 43 got to meet President Richard M. Nixon at the White House. (C)

Chrysler provided this Austin-built, Plymouth-badged Cricket as a "captive import" for Chrysler-Plymouth dealers. Cricket's first year sales only reached 20,000 and, plagued with quality problems, it was dropped after two years. Chrysler offered the Colt and Cricket to counter other imports and U.S.-produced subcompacts Chevrolet Vega and Ford Pinto. (C)

The Chrysler Charger coupe was among a variety of unique models that Chrysler assembled in Australia. Changes for right-hand-drive are seen in both the steering wheel and windshield wiper mountings. Some parts were exported from U.S. or Canadian plants, but most had to be locally manufactured to comply with "local content" laws. By 1973, overseas sales accounted for nearly a third of Chrysler unit sales, but profits were harder to come by. (C)

This publicity photo of a mid-sized '73 Plymouth Satellite wagon is notable for its use of African-American models, a recognition of the growing minority market. Nineteen seventy-three was the all-time peak year for Plymouth production: 882,196. Detroit's fortunes—a record 11.4 million new cars—were to be changed forever by the Arab-Israeli War late that year. The resulting Arab oil embargo doubled energy costs and caused massive disruptions in Detroit. (C)

A 1973 photo illustrates the breadth of Dodge's truck line in the 1970s—pickups to highway tractors. The market for trucks as replacements for passenger cars had not yet developed. Total industry truck production in 1974 came to 2.2 million while cars totaled 8.1 million. In 1999, about the same number of cars, 8.3 million, were produced in North America versus truck output of 9.3 million. (C)

Nineteen seventy-four was the final Model Year for this Barracuda, Chrysler's pony car entry. Production was only 11,734—and peak of 64,596 in '65 was never in a class with Ford's Mustang. Ford salvaged Mustang's name with a downsized 4-cylinder Pinto-based car to satisfy the public's instant demand for economy—but Chrysler had no Four to offer, and was running short of cash to design and tool one. (C)

Among other victims of the first energy crisis were large luxury cars like this 50th Anniversary 1974 Chrysler New Yorker Brougham St. Regis with an unacceptably thirsty 440-cid, 225-hp V-8. Within a few years, government-regulated fuel economy test numbers would be posted on all new cars. Chrysler make sales in 1974 declined to 107,000. (C)

For the first time since before World War II, 1974 saw a return to the Plymouth lineup of vehicles registered as trucks. This Voyager multi-purpose vehicle was the Plymouth version of Dodge's people-transporting van, popular among car poolers, large families and hotel and airport livery services. It offered seating capacities of 5 to 15 passengers. (C)

Plymouth's other "truck" for 1974, this four-wheel-drive Trail Duster—based on the Dodge Ramcharger—was too far ahead of its time: the Sports Utility Vehicle fad didn't sweep the country until 15 years later. This SUV never caught on because the public then was turning from such fun vehicles to strictly economical transportation. In mid-1975 Chrysler began importing the Mitsubishi-built Plymouth Arrow to replace the British Cricket. (C)

Chrysler's new management team, President Eugene A. Cafiero (left) and Chairman John J. Riccardo, are pictured here with the mid-sized 1975 Dodge Charger SE coupe, introduced to counter the Chevrolet Monte Carlo and Ford Thunderbird. Riccardo, a finance man, succeeded Virgil Boyd as president in 1970 and moved up to chairman in 1975 upon Lynn Townsend's retirement. Cafiero (1926–), an industrial engineer, succeeded Riccardo as president. (C)

This was Chrysler's Highland Park headquarters in 1975, a disastrous year for Detroit. Industry sales fell to 8.2 million, lowest since 1964, with imports taking 18 percent of the market. Chrysler's share fell to 12 percent with sales below a million for the first time since 1963. The company introduced cash rebates to move sluggish inventories and, in dire financial condition, sold a new plant it had built in Pennsylvania to Volkswagen. (C)

Big news for 1976 was introduction of "F-bodied" cars to replace the venerable Valiant/Dart family. Shown here is the array of Plymouth Volare bodies—sedan, wagon, and coupe. The Dodge version was named Aspen. These started a series of Plymouths, Dodges, and Chryslers that lasted through the 1989 model. However, in '76 it also put Plymouth and Dodge in the costly position of offering three models on seven different wheelbases. (C)

The first of the Volare/Aspen spin-offs were these 112.7-in wheelbase '77 Chrysler LeBaron models. These were the smallest and lightest Chryslers offered since the original '24 Chrysler. 1977 was last year for full-sized Dodge Monaco and Plymouth Grand Fury models, and the first year that Dodge outsold Plymouth. Chrysler began selling off some of its non-automotive assets—Airtemp, Marine, and real estate—to raise money. (C)

For 1978, Chrysler pioneered the first U.S. cars with transverse-engined front-wheel-drive (FWD) design, Plymouth Horizon and Dodge Omni, shown here in an upscale "wood-grained" model. Only hatchback four-door bodies were offered and fewer than 190,000 '78s were built. Chrysler had to buy the 104.7-cid (1.7-liter) 4-cylinder engine for the cars from Volkswagen. Chrysler share fell to 10 percent, lowest since 1962—in a nearly 11-million-unit car market. (C)

In 1979, Chrysler produced its first spin-offs from the subcompact Omni/Horizon: the sporty two-door Dodge 024 shown here and a companion Plymouth TC3, both on a 96.7-in wheelbase, slightly shorter than the 99.2 of four-door models. Combined Omni/Horizon production topped 300,000 in '79, but compact Aspen/Volare models were Chrysler's top sellers. (C)

With full-sized Dodge and Plymouths no longer in production, Chrysler's fleet sales people successfully enticed the nation's police forces into cars like this '78 Dodge Aspen cruiser photographed in Phoenix, Arizona. Previously, such cars had been considered too small for burly troopers. These Plymouth and Dodge rear-wheel-drive police cars were a roadway staple throughout the '80s despite competition from full-sized Chevrolet and Ford cruisers. (C)

Dodge dealers offered both front-wheel-drive (left) and rear-wheel-drive imported Colt models from Mitsubishi of Japan in 1979. Combined sales of 104,000 were less than domestic Dodge Omni's 142,000, but the imports were important to dealers in certain areas, especially the West and East coasts. Early in 1979, the Iranian Revolution caused a gasoline-availability panic in the U.S., and the public again abandoned larger cars and trucks. (C)

Dodge perfectly captured the trend for trucks as personal transportation as well as utilitarian cargo haulers with the '78 Little Express Truck which came to be known among enthusiasts as "L'il Red Wagon." A 1980 model "recreational vehicle"—the new description—is shown here. (C)

The car-based panel deliveries of the '30s had long been replaced by the 90-in wheelbase "compact trucks" of the '60s (p. 85). Those in turn had grown outside the "compact" envelope as shown here by this B200 Dodge cargo van, available with 109-in or 127-in wheelbase. (C)

This aerodynamic coupe was described as "an advance design of an experimental four passenger electric car being developed by General Electric and Chrysler Corporation for delivery to the U.S. Department of Energy" in 1979. It was to be powered by "high-energy-density" lead-acid batteries. (C)

Nine

THE WHITE KNIGHT
IACOCCA FROM FORD

Lee A. Iacocca, president of Ford Motor Company, was abruptly fired by Henry Ford II in mid-1978. Iacocca was soon approached by Chrysler Chairman John Riccardo, who explained that Chrysler was in a financial crisis and needed his help. Iacocca joined Chrysler in November as president, replacing Eugene Cafiero. Riccardo retired in 1979 and Iacocca succeeded him as chairman. Soon this "White Knight," father of numerous product and marketing brainstorms, had gathered around him a team of trusted former Ford executives—the "Gang of Ford." But even after selling many of Chrysler's remaining assets, the company remained in desperate straits. Share dropped to 9 percent in 1979, then to 7 percent in 1980—an historical low—when Chrysler's car sales totaled only 625,000, lowest in a regular production year since 1938. Chrysler needed loans to launch new models that would save it, but bankers weren't interested. (N)

Chrysler's salvation came from a massive $1.5 billion Federal Loan Guarantee, devised by a combination of corporate management, union leadership, Carter administration officials, and Congressmen from both parties. Here, on January 7, 1980, Iacocca signed the agreement as government officials witnessed. UAW President Douglas Fraser, who joined Chrysler's Board of Directors in an unprecedented alliance, is at right. President Jimmy Carter is third from right. (C)

Short of cash and needing to concentrate on just cars and light trucks, by the early 1980s Chrysler discontinued heavy trucks (p. 97) and sold its long-treasured Defense Division, which included tanks like this Abrams undergoing tests before production start-up. Space Division had declined to nothing and most of Chrysler's overseas operations also had been sold. Production ceased at the aged Hamtramck and Lynch Road plants in 1980. (C)

106

Chrysler's motive for re-introducing, after a six-year hiatus, the limited-production Imperial line as a sleek two-door coupe for 1981 (top) was perhaps the desire to have an upscale car to compete with the Lincoln Mark series and the Cadillac Eldorado. It was built—for only three model years with a total output of 10,981—on the mid-sized Cordoba's 112.7-in wheelbase. Nineteen eighty-one was the final year for Chrysler's full-sized, rear-wheel-drive Newport sedans (center) on the 118.5-in wheelbase. LeBaron was Chrysler's lowest series for 1981, a rear-wheel-drive car which in its most dressed up form was this Town & Country wagon (bottom). (C)

What Iacocca and Chrysler so cleverly teased (p. 4) long before production started was the boxy, front-wheel-drive, six-passenger K-car, here (top) as a 1981 Plymouth Reliant. This and the sister Dodge Aries were based on an enlarged FWD platform from the Omni/Horizon of 1978, with essentially the same 99.6-in wheelbase. A seemingly endless family of derivatives evolved from the K. Among the first was the '82 Chrysler LeBaron convertible (center), the first American regular-production convertible since Cadillac had issued its "last" in 1976. In 1983, both Chrysler and Dodge marketed three-inch-longer-wheelbase K's, seen here (bottom) as a Dodge 600 ES. (C)

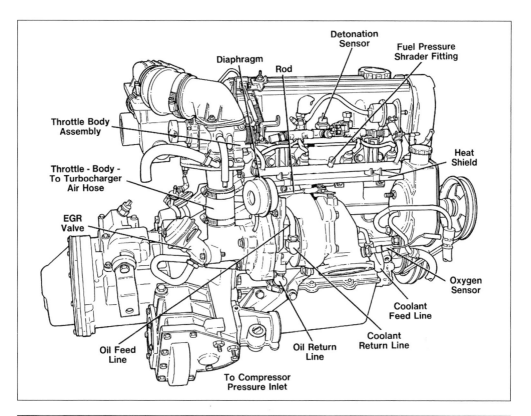

Detonation Sensor

Fuel Pressure Shrader Fitting

Diaphragm

Rod

Throttle Body Assembly

Throttle - Body - To Turbocharger Air Hose

Heat Shield

EGR Valve

Oxygen Sensor

Oil Feed Line

Oil Return Line

Coolant Feed Line

Coolant Return Line

To Compressor Pressure Inlet

Chrysler's K-cars initially were powered by the company's own new 2.2-l/135-cid 84-hp overhead-cam Four, the first 4-cylinder since the Maxwell-derived engine of the '32 Plymouth. An optional 2.6-l/156-cid Four was imported from Mitsubishi. For 1984, Chrysler powered up its Four with turbo-charging, illustrated by the cutaway drawing (top). The Turbo produced 140 hp, and powered this sporty version of the K, an '84 Dodge Daytona Turbo (bottom), mounted on a slightly shorter 97-in wheelbase. (C)

109

Chrysler's priciest standard K-car for '84 was this $16,495 LeBaron Town & Country convertible (top) with imitation wood-grain station wagon trim. The photo is notable for the swimsuit model, about the last of "cheesecake" publicity photos in the new world of female executives. The furthest stretch of a K-car was the $21,975 seven-passenger, divider-window Chrysler Executive limousine (bottom). It was based on an extended 131-inch wheelbase and used the front-wheel-drive 101-hp Mitsubishi 2.6-l engine. A five-passenger Executive sedan on a 124-in wheelbase also was sold. The Executives were off-line conversions from Chrysler's St. Louis, Missouri, assembly plant. (C)

If the economical K-car was what saved Chrysler Corporation, the greatest of its derivatives, the Minivan, is what made it a ton of money. The FWD-based Minivan had its inception about 1974 across town under Harold K. Sperlich (1929–), then Ford's product planning vice president. But Ford had no domestic FWD powerpack available and none planned. Sperlich was fired by Henry Ford II and hired by Chrysler where he became an intermediary in the recruitment of Iacocca. By that time Chrysler had FWD in production and plans underway for the K cars. The Dodge Caravan and Plymouth Voyager Minivans were introduced in the fall of 1983 as '84 models. They had a sensational and lasting effect on the American market. The company earned a profit of $2.4 billion in 1984 and Chrysler remains Minivan market leader after 17 years. Chrysler Chairman Lee Iacocca is shown here being filmed for a Minivan television commercial. (C)

1985 DODGE PRODUCT LINE

Dodge Cars

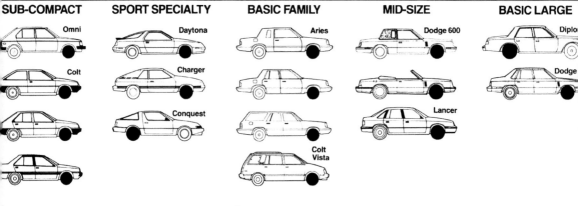

SUB-COMPACT	SPORT SPECIALTY	BASIC FAMILY	MID-SIZE	BASIC LARGE
Omni	Daytona	Aries	Dodge 600	Diplo[...]
Colt	Charger			Dodge
	Conquest		Lancer	
		Colt Vista		

Dodge Trucks

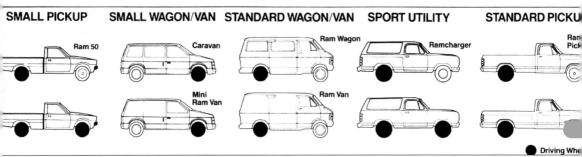

SMALL PICKUP	SMALL WAGON/VAN	STANDARD WAGON/VAN	SPORT UTILITY	STANDARD PICKU[...]
Ram 50	Caravan	Ram Wagon	Ramcharger	Ram Pick[...]
	Mini Ram Van	Ram Van		

● Driving Whe[...]

This 1985 Model Year advertisement shows, with FWD and RWD being designated by wheel shading, the full range of cars and trucks then being sold by Dodge dealers. Plymouth passenger car sales that year were less than those of Chrysler for the first time, because Chryslers had been downsized into Plymouth's traditional entry-level size and economy but presented a more prestigious nameplate. The Plymouth Voyager Minivan was counted as a truck rather than a car. The U.S. auto industry had survived a recession in the early '80s with a 7.8 million-year and import share of 30 percent. Car sales had recovered by mid-decade to a nearly 11-million level with the import share slightly less. (C)

Oddly, group photographs of the "Gang of Ford" seem to be nonexistent in public archives. This picture taken at the Washington Press Club in 1983 shows three of them and their key outside allies, from left to right, Gerald Greenwald (1935–), Doug Fraser of the UAW, Iaccoca, Senator Don Riegle, Sperlich, and Michigan Governor Jim Blanchard. The first executive Iaccoca lured from Ford was Paul Bergmoser (1916–), Ford's purchasing vice president, who served as president of Chrysler 1979–1981. There was no one in the Chrysler presidency from 1981 to 1984. Then Sperlich filled the position for two years. In 1985 a separate company was formed for vehicle manufacturing and sales, Chrysler Motors, of which Sperlich was president and Greenwald chairman, 1985–1988. They were succeeded 1988–1990 by Robert A. Lutz (1932–) as president and Bennett E. Bidwell (1927–) as chairman, all former Ford executives. Iaccoca remained chairman of the corporation. (R)

Its pockets full of Minivan cash, Chrysler again went on a spending spree, just as it had in the '60s. In 1985, it bought corporate jet aircraft maker Gulfstream Aerospace. A U.S. Air Force Gulfstream used to transport government VIPs is pictured here. Gulfstream was sold in 1989 when, as before, Chrysler faced financial problems from declining automotive sales. (G)

Chrysler's 1987 purchase of American Motors Corporation (AMC) was its best deal. AMC, formed from Nash and Hudson in 1954, had purchased Jeep from Kaiser in 1970. When Chrysler bought AMC, it gained Jeep and several plants including the dated but productive Toledo, Ohio, Jeep plant shown here. (C)

Willys-Overland (p. 29) made its lasting contribution in World War II supplying the famed "1/4-ton truck, General Purpose" whose "GP" initials American soldiers soon converted to "Jeep." These American troops are struggling to push a Jeep through heavy snow late in 1944 during the Battle of the Budge. (C)

114

Willys continued building the Jeep as this CJ—for "civilian jeep"—model after the war. Jeep had become a worldwide symbol, perhaps more than anything else, of American power and the industry's Arsenal of Democracy. Jeep name and styling became one of motordom's most valued trademarks. (C)

For the post-war civilian passenger car market, Willys introduced this all steel '46 Jeep Station Wagon, again styled like the Army version. Never a huge sales success, it took some 40 years for this grandparent of the SUV to impact the market. (C)

With AMC, Chrysler also gained another car line, Eagle, and a third dealer body, Jeep-Eagle. By this time, the venerable domestic AMC Rambler had been replaced by French-designed, North American-built Eagle-branded Renaults, such as this '88 Eagle Premier which joined the Chrysler family. (C)

Chrysler ended the '80s once again in the soup with rapidly declining profits as industry volume shrunk. The 1989 Model Year was the last for its aged RWD V-8-powered cars like this Chrysler Fifth Avenue (top), the Dodge Diplomat and Plymouth Gran Fury. The renamed Dodge Spirit (shown in front of the "Spirit of Detroit" sculpture at Detroit's City County Building) was a less boxy K-car. Chrysler also imported, unsuccessfully, a Maserati sports roadster (bottom) from Italy. (C)

Ten

GLOBALIZATION

As the final decade for Chrysler as an independent American business icon dawned, the company was building this spectacular new headquarters some 20 miles north of Highland Park in suburban Auburn Hills, Michigan. When Chrysler offices and operations started moving to the new facility between 1992 and 1998, the collection of Highland Park buildings, new and old, began to be torn down. Meanwhile, Chrysler again fell into financial crises with losses of $795 million in 1991 and $2.6 billion in 1993—but a host of brilliant new products were under development and major management changes were soon to occur. The pressures of globalization ultimately convinced Chrysler it could not compete on a now-necessary worldwide basis without an international partner. Chrysler would merge with Daimler-Benz of Germany before the '90s ended. (D)

Before Lee Iacocca turned over the reins to new management at the end of 1992, he put his stamp of approval on Chrysler's first truly all-new cars in a decade. These were the sensational "cab-forward" design LH cars that provided more interior room under their sleek skins and were powered by new V-6 engines. Here Iacocca, 68, poses for the 1991 Annual Report with a prototype of the '94 top-of-the-line LHS. (A)

Chrysler's new management team, from left to right, Executive Vice Presidents Thomas G. Denomme and Jerome B. York, Chairman Robert J. Eaton (1940–), and President Robert A. Lutz posed here for the 1992 Annual Report. Eaton was recruited from GM for the post and the others were Ford veterans. York, the chief financial officer, later left for a position with major Chrysler investor Kirk Kerkorian who had teamed with Iacocca in a bizarre attempt to take over the company. (A)

The new 113-inch wheelbase LH sedans, such as this Dodge Intrepid, introduced the industry to both cab-forward body engineering and "platform management," a new team-design concept. Chrysler practiced platform management on its subsequent new models and it was adopted by major competitors as well. The LH cars were a significant 5 inches wider than the K-car-based upscale Dodge and Chrysler models they replaced. (F)

A typical instrument panel of the 1990s is illustrated by this '93 Dodge Intrepid. Safety airbags are mounted in the horn pad of the steering wheel and the right side of the padded dash. (F)

The most impressive version of Chrysler's cab-forward styling and efficient body design was introduced with the '95 Neon. Whether badged Dodge or Plymouth and two-door or four-door, it provided exceptional rear-seat knee and leg room for a subcompact car. (F)

The late-20th century descendant of the World-War-II Jeep is the utilitarian Jeep Wrangler, which still shows many of the styling cues and the practicality of the original. Wranglers were especially popular with youthful drivers, male and female. (F)

Chrysler had three entries in the wagon-like Sports Utility Vehicle field in the '90s: the straight-sided "carry-over" Jeep Cherokee, this modernized upscale '95 Grand Cherokee and the Ram-based Dodge Durango. (F)

After languishing far behind Ford and Chevrolet in truck sales, Dodge had a smash hit with the new "highway hauler" front-end styling introduced with its '94 models like the Ram pictured. The same design was applied to full-sized Ram and compact Dakota trucks as well as the Durango SUV. (D)

The Dodge V-10-powered Viper sports car was introduced in 1992 as an image builder. Chairman Bob Eaton, left, and President Bob Lutz pose here with one. The $50,000-plus sports car only had modest sales but brought considerable prestige to the company while attracting customers to Dodge showrooms. (F)

The Plymouth Prowler, shown here in pre-production form, was a "far-out" show car that amazingly made it into limited production at $35,000 a copy in the '90s. It was Chrysler's first stab at the "retro" market. (D)

Ironically, Prowler most resembled a '32 Ford Street Rod rather than a vintage Chrysler product. This was not surprising since Chrysler Design Vice President (later EVP) Tom Gale had among his personal collection just such a car. Gale is pictured here with his vintage Ford at a car show. (D)

Corporate product planning called for an LH car to be offered by each dealer body. Here (top) is a '95 Eagle Vision (C). Like the Dodge Intrepid, Chrysler Concorde, and LHS versions, it was offered only in a four-door sedan—the many different body styles of the past had come down to just one for the company's large cars. Station wagons had been eliminated in favor of Minivans and SUVs. In 1998, Chrysler announced discontinuance of the Eagle line and elimination of the third dealer body. The remaining dealer bodies were (center) Chrysler-Plymouth-Jeep (D) and (bottom) Dodge-Dodge Truck (D). That arrangement was also to change within a few years.

The old East Jefferson Plant, at various times in the Chrysler Heritage the home of Thomas-Detroit, Chalmers, Chrysler ,and Chrysler-Plymouth, was demolished in 1991 to make way for a huge new facility on Detroit's east side. The Chalmers buildings (p. 19) can be readily identified here in the background. Dodge Main fell victim earlier to the wrecking ball, to clear land for a new Cadillac plant straddling the Detroit-Hamtramck line. (C)

Chrysler's new Jefferson North Plant, shown here, was the major new company construction project in Detroit in the final decade of the 20th century. It was erected north of the old East Jefferson Plant to build Jeep Grand Cherokee models. Of Chrysler's original Detroit area assembly plants, only McGraw Glass (DeSoto) was still operating as part of the company. (C)

By the 1990s, automotive assembly techniques had become highly automated, as illustrated by this view of the robotized welding of the entire body side of a Jeep Grand Cherokee at the new Jefferson North plant. It required an entirely different design and expensive tooling while producing more consistent quality and greater efficiency. Welders were now machine operators. (C)

Chrysler had no viable competitors in the Minivan market for a decade after the vehicle's late '83 introduction. When Chrysler finally introduced a completely updated Minivan for '96, it trumped competitors with a "four-door" model, shown here. By the beginning of the century, however, competition in the field had become fierce, and Chrysler Minivan volume suffered. (C)

This 108-in wheelbase, mid-sized Plymouth Breeze, introduced for 1996 and preceded by similar Dodge Stratus and Chrysler Cirrus models, could be termed the last Plymouth automobile. Chrysler announced in 2000 that it would phase out the Plymouth nameplate after more than 60 years. By now, cars and minivans branded as Chryslers more than covered the market served by Chrysler-Plymouth-Jeep dealers—who would have to endure yet another sign change. (A)

This sleek 1998 model Chrysler LHS marked the second generation of the company's large car offerings, accompanied by Chrysler Concorde, Chrysler 300, and Dodge Intrepid models, all four-door sedans. But it was the terminal year for Chrysler Corporation as an independent American company, as a highly trumpeted "merger of equals" with Daimler-Benz of Germany was concluded late in the year. (F)

Chrysler's 106-in wheelbase Sebring convertible, shown here at introduction of the second-generation 2001 model, became the industry's biggest selling convertible in 1996 with annual sales over 50,000. Sebrings originally were built at the one-time joint venture Chrysler/Mitsubishi Diamond-Star Motors plant in Normal, Illinois. For this new model, production was transferred to the Cirrus/Stratus Chrysler plant in Sterling Heights, Michigan. (F)

Chrysler's "retro" Neon-based PT Cruiser was the brainchild of Bob Lutz, and a follow-up to the auto show popularity of the Plymouth Prowler (p. 121). It looked like a '37 Ford Street Rod and gained "Car of the Year" recognition after its introduction in mid-2000—even though PT Cruisers were registered as trucks for Federal fuel-economy standards. Production could not keep up with demand in Chrysler's closing volley of the century. (F)

Chrysler's illustrious heritage as an American vehicle maker ended on November 17, 1998, after stockholders approved a merger with Germany's Daimler-Benz—termed at the time a "marriage made in heaven." Chrysler brought a rich purse to the nuptials—profits totaling $12 billion in the four years preceding the merger. The surviving entity was DaimlerChrysler AG, a German corporation that was supposed to combine globally the best of Mercedes engineering and quality with Chrysler's reputation for ingenious product planning, speedy decision-making, and efficient development and manufacturing. But the two company's stars, Chrysler's five-pointer (top) and Mercedes' three-pointer, seemed crossed. Veteran Chrysler executives left the new company. Lacking experience in the American mass-market, German management fired two American Chrysler presidents, Tom Stallkamp and Jim Holden, in less than two years. Late in 2000, DaimlerChrysler Chairman Jüergen E. Schrempp injudiciously told a London newspaper that, despite public pronouncements to the contrary, the "merger" had been simply a takeover by the German company. As the new millennium opened in 2001, the future of the enterprise was once again in doubt. Chrysler Group profits crashed as market share declined. DaimlerChrysler reacted with a series of production line and staff cutbacks, adjusting to the lower market share and vigorous competition from import companies.(D)

ACKNOWLEDGMENTS

I wish to acknowledge the assistance of the following, knowing that I probably have forgotten some, from whom I beg forgiveness: Sam Bono, Laura Corwin, Bob Cosgrove, Karen Day, Lou DeSimone, Barry Dressel, Tom Featherstone, Ted Flynn, Barbara Fronczak, Larry Gustin, Charles Hanson, Mark Harvey, Charlie Hyde, Jack Kausch, Walt McCall, Janet Mendler, Keith Mordoff, Patience Nauta, Mark Patrick, Art Ponder, Frank Rhodes Jr., Steven Rossi, Carole Royer, Dawn Shoskes, Marty Skrocki, Pauline Testerman, Gene Weiss, and Doug Williams. Their contributions ranged from a little to a lot. To my wife Karen goes a special bouquet for her patience—and editing skills.